FAIR EXCHANGE

"Finney" as seen at horse events the world over. *From the painting by Heinrich von Michaelis.*

FAIR EXCHANGE

Recollections
of a Life
With Horses

by

HUMPHREY S. FINNEY

with

Raleigh Burroughs

CHARLES SCRIBNER'S SONS
New York

Library of Congress Cataloging in Publication Data
Finney, Humphrey S
    Fair exchange; recollections of a life with horses.

    Autobiography.
    1. Finney, Humphrey S   2. Horsemen—
Correspondence, reminiscences, etc.   3. Horse buying.
I. Burroughs, Raleigh, joint author.   II. Title.
SF33.F56A33   798.4′092′4   73–1339
ISBN 0–684–13707–0

1 3 5 7 9 11 13 15 17 19 H/C 20 18 16 14 12 10 8 6 4 2

Printed in the United States of America

To Olive

without whose support and encouragement, much of what I have written about would not have taken place

CONTENTS

FOREWORD

Where and when does a book really begin? The people who have suggested at one time or another to Humphrey Finney that he chronicle his life in book form are legion; each must now share in some way the satisfaction or frustration of the end-product. But this book really began several years ago when Bill Steinkraus, sometime stock analyst, concert violist, and editor—and longtime captain and star performer of the United States Equestrian Team, presented himself to Finney as an old friend in a new role, that of potential publisher.

As a result of their discussions, Finney was soon actively in search of a suitable collaborator, and after several false starts his search was rewarded by another old friend, Raleigh Burroughs. Finney and Burroughs had been acquainted for nearly forty years, during which time Raleigh had been successively a racing writer and editor of *Turf and Sport Digest* and *The Maryland Horse,* and a racing columnist of rare humor and insight for *The Chronicle of the Horse* and other publications. Raleigh knew Finney and his era, and most of the horses, events, and people who had been significant in Finney's life.

During the period that the manuscript was taking shape, Bill Steinkraus changed positions and was obliged personally to give up the project, which he did reluctantly and only after interesting Scribners in its publication.

Through all this formative process I have been an anxious and interested onlooker. From the outset I shared with Bill Steinkraus the conviction that the horse world in general and the Thoroughbred industry in particular would be very much losers if some part of Humphrey Finney's knowledge and insight was not recorded for posterity. For half a century Finney has seen, known, and in many cases been an active participant in the most significant events involving the horse in this country and abroad; the principal actors, human and equine, are or have been his friends and acquaintances.

But my interest in this book goes well beyond that. Since I began working directly for and with Finney nearly twenty-five years ago, we have enjoyed a rapport and relationship which is extremely rare between father and son, because few fathers are such rare and exceptional human beings. His total mastery of his chosen work, his honesty, his humanity, his humor—all have impressed me, touched me, and enriched my life; and I hope this book will convey these qualities in some part to those who have known Finney only slightly, or perhaps not at all.

John M. S. Finney

Greenwich, 1973

FAIR EXCHANGE

ONE

To Be With Horses

When I came to America from England in 1921, I came first class —on a freighter. The S.S. *Mercian* was not so posh as the lamented *Lusitania,* nor so swift, but I had my own comfortable cabin and an opportunity to learn something of the mores of the States during the fourteen-day voyage.

Besides a load of fertilizer and myself, the cargo consisted of my luggage, my treasured horse books, two homeward-bound cattlemen who had been escorting livestock to Liverpool, and an earthy American traveling salesman. Furthermore, a load of gold bullion was rumored to be stashed in a mystery cabin which was always kept locked and under surveillance. The rumor was never confirmed, but the idea added some excitement to the adventure.

My shipboard companions patiently answered the multitude of questions I put to them regarding the country that was to become my home, and offered much unsolicited advice and information. The traveling man introduced me to the vagaries of the American language. He warned me against the use of certain words and combinations of words, particularly the popular four-word Yankee hyphenation that alludes to canine ancestry on the dam's side.

"Those are shooting words!" the American declared. "When you use that expression, you want to duck. It means fight!"

I suppose I should have been awed when the *Mercian* sailed into New York harbor, but I don't believe I was. The Statue of Liberty represented opportunity to me, though, as it still does to all immigrants reaching America; but I had no vague plans for better living or for making a fortune. My objective was more explicit: I was being offered the chance to spend the rest of my life with horses.

When the ship docked, my salesman acquaintance went down the gangplank before me. As he stepped onto the pier, another man rushed toward him. My language teacher dropped his bag and yelled in surprise, "Well, look who's here to meet me! Why you old son-of-a-bitch!"

The shooting words!

I didn't wait for the gun play, but dived behind a stack of baggage to wait until the bullets stopped flying. But no shots were fired and, when I deemed it safe, I peeped out. The friendly traveling salesman was almost convulsed with laughter. When he calmed down enough to talk, he explained that bloodshed did not always follow the unflattering combination of words. It was, he said, a matter of facial expression and vocal inflection. In the years since, I have added many Americanisms to my vocabulary, with inflections, and have found them useful.

Debarking, I was attired in a manner I considered fitting for a horsey English gentleman: rough tweeds, derby, and cream-colored pin-striped vest. A stout walking stick lent a touch of swagger—I hoped. Not visible were my full-length heavy woolen undergarments, which had been comfortable enough in Britain, but were a trifle warm for May 7 in New York.

At eighteen I looked to the future with a feeling of pleasant anticipation and confidence. And why shouldn't I? My purse contained the American equivalent of 46 guineas, and a position with horses awaited me in Michigan, a place a few shires away from Manhattan. Also, I had been told that in this land of promise a man could rub a horse or act as chambermaid to one without being marked as a third-class citizen.

And in many respects it seemed that my life to that point had been lived in anticipation of this opportunity—to spend full time with horses.

I was born at Rusholme, near Manchester, England, in the County Palatine of Lancashire, on October 25, 1902. I was the second oldest of the five children, three boys and two girls, of William Henry and Laura Stone Finney. At the time my father, an Anglican clergyman, was assisting *his* father of the same name, who had the living of Christ Church, Rusholme. We lived on Heald Place, in a small row house.

I have been told that my vocal powers were of stakes class, even in infancy. A legend of the neighborhood had it that when I raised my voice in protest or in pain of colic, would-be sleepers nearby slammed their windows shut.

My father stemmed from an old Staffordshire family, with a tradition in the church. He had been an excellent cricketer, and had "stroked the boat" at Oxford in the early nineties. He was also a fine tennis player, and spent many hours—when it wasn't raining—working on his own tennis lawn.

Law was the profession of my mother's family. Many of her kin were Derbyshire lawyers. Mother was very proud of the fact that her grandmother was the daughter of the Earl of Derby. That is the reason Stanley, the Derby family name, is in the names of her children and grandchildren. My middle name is Stanley, and my son, John Michael, and one of my two daughters, Laura Marguerite, are also Stanleys.

Father and Mother had both been associated with that great humanitarian, Dr. Thomas Barnardo, who gave refuge to waifs and strays of all ages in the East End of London. Above the doors of Dr. Barnardo's Homes were the words: "No destitute child ever refused admission." And so it was. The Homes did wonderful work in lifting poor kids from London's slums and guiding them to better lives.

Father was Dr. Barnardo's chaplain as a young man, and Mother, a trained nurse, was matron of "Babies' Castle," Dr. Barnardo's Home in Hawkeshurst, Kent, for children up to seven years of age.

In 1904, Father became vicar of St. Mary's Church in Rawtenstall, also in Lancashire, so we moved there. When I was seven, I was sent off, with my brother Claud, who was a year older, to board at Winterdyne School at Southport. For a time I suffered from homesickness, but the attack must have immunized me because in the half-dozen decades since I never have been bothered by the ailment.

My father became rector of St. Margaret's Church, Burnage, in 1913, and held that post until long after I left England in 1921. While at Burnage I attended the second oldest public school in England, the Manchester Grammar School, founded in 1515 by Hugh Oldham, Bishop of Exeter. The sainted Bishop's motto was *Sapere aude* (Dare to be wise). I did not put forth a driving effort in search of wisdom; rather, I breezed along with an absolute minimum of effort. My lack of diligence qualified me for membership in a backward grade known as "slackers' rest." As the lads in my class were older and bigger than the "bright" kids at the same scholastic level, we were masters on the sporting fields. It was satisfying to triumph at contact sports and tug-of-war over boys who were getting higher marks. Most of my classmates and I were merely "serving our time" until we could leave school.

It was my grandfather Finney who introduced me to the wonderful world of the horse. He was the old-fashioned type of country parson who might have come right out of the pages of Trollope or Surtees. He loved everything about the English countryside—the people, the horses, the wayside taverns—and he was a part of it all. Besides, he was shrewd enough to realize that riding behind stylish horses could be profitable to a man who bred a few, and it was better than pedaling a tricycle. He cut quite a figure driving a high-stepping hackney around the country, ever spreading the word of God and selling a horse now and then. I picked up some knowledge of both fields, but my dream of heaven at that time was to be with my grandfather and his horses. When I had advanced far enough to take the reins myself, I felt I had attained paradise. A lad with a sports car or a motorcycle today is no more lord of the road than was Finney with the reins in his hands sixty years earlier.

When I was about ten or twelve, I visited a Cheshire clergyman who owned a gig—a high two-wheeled vehicle. I prevailed upon the preacher's son to take me for a drive and, better yet, to let me take the reins. He assumed that I knew what I was doing.

The entrance to the driveway was guarded by two posts and beside each post was a large stone to protect it from wheel hubs. I started off well and was going at a nice speed approaching the exit. The horse got through all right, but one wheel went over a stone and my passenger and I went flying. I dislocated my shoulder and broke the small bone on top of that joint.

If my father had hoped that I would follow in the family tradition and sign up with the church, he was disappointed. It was early apparent that my inclinations, and whatever talents I might have, could not lead me into the office of village vicar without jeopardizing the structure of the Church of England.

When I got my first glimpse of a Thoroughbred, I decided that here was Nature's handsomest gift to man. I bought books on the breed and learned about the Godolphin Barb, the Byerly Turk and the Darley Arabian when other youngsters were absorbing the complexities of plane geometry—as I should have been. No child in Sunday school could reel off the names (and dates) of as many Epsom Derby winners as I, and no student in day classes could better explain the importance of the broodmare in production. By the time I was fourteen or fifteen, I had visited every stock farm within walking or driving distance of home.

Horse sales and races drew my interest, too. My schoolmasters began to notice a coincidence between my absence from classes and the dates of race meetings and sales in the vicinity. Once when I was marked "present" on the day of an important turf event, a member of the faculty asked, "May I assume that the races were called off?"

I managed to struggle along in the academic world and my father was still hopeful that I might come to some good when I was finally freed from Manchester Grammar School in 1917. As horses dominated my thinking, my father decided that the only sensible course was to send me to the Agricultural College at Preston. I got in because the vice-president and my father had been close friends in college. This was fine, but I still spent considerable time away from classes.

At the College I became good friends with Mr. Charles Blackhurst, M.R.C.V.S. (Member of the Royal College of Veterinary Surgeons), a skilled veterinarian. (In England, a vet or a dentist or a surgeon was addressed as "mister," not "doctor.") Mr. Blackhurst was a first-class horseman, and had the confidence of farmers and breeders and the respect of other men in his profession.

With him, I traveled to the farms, watching him treat the injured and ailing animals. The privilege of acting as aide to a superior practitioner exposed me to many of the problems faced by a practical horseman—experience that could not have been bought at any price. Mr. Blackhurst lectured on veterinary science at the Agricultural College, but I learned more about care and management and veterinary practices traveling with him than I ever did in class.

I wonder today at the man's patience—performing his work and answering the questions of a compulsively interested youngster. Perhaps it was because he understood my interest that he was so liberal with his time and knowledge.

I was fascinated by draft horses. Their heroic size and innate power won my admiration and affection. In those days, horses represented motor power for everything that had to be dragged, so the big ones were of prime importance to a country's economy. Much of Mr. Blackhurst's practice was with the draft breeds.

I read Professor Wortley-Axe's *The Horse*—nine volumes, published early in this century. The series showed diagrams, sketches and photographs of horses of all breeds, explaining what was good conformation and what was bad. Another book I treasured was by General Fitz-Wygram. Also titled *The Horse,* it was of even earlier origin. Because the material contained in these books was so interesting to me, much of it stayed with me, and I still have both books fifty-five years later. This reading, coupled with the study of actual cases with Mr. Blackhurst, gave me an education I could not have obtained in any other way, and I got it painlessly and without conscious effort.

My main complaint with the Agricultural College was that the professors insisted upon wasting my time and theirs on subjects that had nothing to do with horses, or animals of any kind. One day in March, 1921 I expressed my resentment by going to Liverpool instead of to classes. It was Grand National Day at Aintree, and a very happy time for me—well worth sacrificing a couple of days of study.

It was my first and only viewing of the Grand National, and it was one of the rare times when the winner of this searching race came home alone. Thirty-odd horses started, but only a half dozen were still up after the first circuit. Shaun Spadah, a great Irish gelding, with that brilliant rider Fred Rees in the saddle, and Mr. Harry Brown on The Bore went the next mile or so as a team. Then The Bore tired and fell and Shaun Spadah cantered home alone at juicy odds before an immense crowd, which included the Prince of Wales and other royalty.

My defection from classes inspired the dean to pen a few lines to my sire. He reported that Finney *filius* had set a new course record for days absent, with another term to go, and had long since lowered the mark for lack of interest in class work. In conclusion, he predicted that the morale of the institution would begin to show a definite upward swing should my association therewith be terminated.

The dean's letter brought on a conference between my father and me, with my father doing the talking. He showed me a letter from an expatriate English clergyman, telling of the opportunities the New World offered a young man. Then he pointed out that he and the dean had been lifelong friends, "and," he added, "I should like to keep it that way."

Blind Tom could see the handwriting on the wall. Only a month later, I stepped off the *Mercian* in New York to begin my professional life with horses.

TWO

Apprenticeship

At the farm in Michigan, I unpacked my heavy tweeds, dozens of wool socks, six pairs of long drawers and seventy-five pounds of books. I doubt that the volume of my luggage has ever been matched by a youth embarking upon a career of farm labor anywhere.

It was a "mixed" farm, but there were some horses. The starting salary was $20 a month in the summer and $10 in the winter, plus board. Aside from the fifteen to sixteen hours a day I was required to devote to farm work, my time was my own. The only trouble was that the farmer, to use another Americanism I learned early, was a little slow with a buck.

One day, after about a year on the job, I accompanied my employer to town where he planned to peddle a load of hogs. When the sale was made, I requested my back pay and, at the same time, handed in my resignation.

"You can't quit!" the farmer said. "Not after I've carried you all winter [at 33⅓ cents a day], and you're just getting to be useful to me."

I reminded him that his ancestors had fought and bled to make America a free country and that the right to quit was one of the freedoms. So I quit. I still have $60 in back wages coming to me, plus interest, which by now should be a tidy sum.

On April 15, 1922, I received a letter from Mr. Jacob DeGeus, manager of the Owosso Sugar Company's Prairie Farm at Alicia, Michigan, about an application I had made. "If you have not taken up a steady position," it said, "we can offer you one so that you may get a start at once. We are not boarding our employees, we only provide them with rooms free of charge. Your board will have to be paid by yourself wherever you are boarding. There are good places here to get board.

"We will pay you $60 per month and we will place you in one of our horse barns. If you accept this offer, please let us hear from you at once, as you can start any time."

I took the job. It tripled my income, even though my outgo was quadrupled.

The sugar company bred and exhibited Belgian draft horses and some Belgian and Percheron grades. The latter were by purebred stallions out of mares of varied parentage. I showed the stock in many places—Syracuse, Chicago, Detroit, Columbus, Des Moines, and Hamline, Minnesota. Some of the horses were superb individuals and won many championships and the accompanying ribbons and trophies.

The draft horse, sad to say, is seen less and less frequently in the modern era. Trucks and power-driven machinery, which don't eat hay when they're idle, have shoved him right out of the picture. The few that remain are in the hands of well-to-do fanciers, who are striving, against great odds, to preserve the several draft breeds.

The draft horses we still see are superior individuals, because they are the only ones retained. The famous Clydesdales that pull Anheuser-Busch's big beer wagon are classic specimens. The St. Louis brewing company breeds them and culls them, presenting only the best in exhibitions and in its advertising. Watching them is a treat to any man who has an affection for the giants of the equine family. They're great action horses, with wonderful shoulders and near-perfect underpinning. They're beautiful!

After two years at Owosso, I began to feel that I was getting somewhere. But despite my fondness for the draft horses, something was tugging me in the direction of the light-horse breeds, so when I was offered a job by Karmar Stables at Blue Ash, Ohio, near Cincinnati, I joined that outfit.

Karmar was owned by Albert Krippendorf, a Cincinnati businessman. He started a stable of show horses, hunters and polo ponies in 1922, and named his stable by using the first syllables of his daughters' names, Karlina and Mary Belle. He also built the Cincinnati Polo Club stable on the ground that later became the site of Lunken Airport.

Albert G. Woodcock, another transplanted Englishman, was the manager of Karmar. He was a fine rider and a first-class horseman—none better. In his youth he was a jockey, after apprenticeship with the well-known Newmarket trainer Bob Sherwood. Both his father and grandfather had been trainers. From Woodcock I learned how to groom a horse—knowledge that should be in the repertoire of every person who shows horses or presents them for sale.

Woodcock bought hunter prospects down at Lexington, Kentucky, principally from a dealer named "Mode" Nichols. I went along on these trips and learned. Woodcock, of course, did the buying, but I watched to see what he bought and tried to figure out why.

I remember one mare he bought that turned out very well. She was a chestnut named Necessity, foaled about 1922. She wasn't listed in the stud book, but was in the appendix. (At that time horses with holes in their pedigrees were registered "for racing purposes only.") Necessity was by Abe Frank, a Remount stallion, out of Omar Wood, by a grandson of Boston. She was about three or four years old when I first saw her. Though small, she had wonderful quality, and was about the same color chestnut as Equipoise; and she had a beautiful, sweet disposition. Just off the racetrack, she was very thin. She had no racing ability at all, but under Woodcock's care and tutelage she became an outstanding conformation lady's hunter. The knack of seeing the potential in an unfurnished racecourse failure has turned a tidy profit for many horsemen developing hunters for the show ring.

Sam McBride was another one we picked up. He was a Thoroughbred right off the track and had won two or three cheap races. By Exterminator's sire McGee and out of a Garry Herman mare, he was big and overgrown, but he had a great shoulder, something that appealed to us.

When we got Sam McBride we found that he was a weak horse, in spite of his structure. It took two years to develop him into a useful mount. The horse would fall over the bloody fence every time we'd take him out, and then we'd have to hose and blister him for a few more months. Finally, he really came to himself and we had a top-class show horse. What probably attracted Woodcock to him in the first place was his excellent shoulder; besides, he was "deep through the heart" and had a nice disposition. But without our extreme patience and perseverance he would have amounted to nothing.

Another Thoroughbred Woodcock picked up was Dominican, by Predicateur, out of Love Apple, by Chuctanunda. Bred in France by General Stephen Sanford, Dominican started life as a political exile. Sanford owned Hurricana Stud, at Amsterdam, New York, as well as a farm in France, and when racing was knocked out in New York in 1910 he sent his horses, including Dominican's dam, overseas. Chuctanunda was the best miler in the East when Dick Welles was the star of the West. (In those days, the West was Cincinnati, Latonia, Louisville, and Lexington. There was good racing too at Nashville, Memphis, and of course at New Orleans.)

Dominican was a great, strong heavyweight horse, tremendously thick through the body and heavy-boned. He toed in a little, but he had great balance. He was a sensational jumper, and could carry any burden put upon him.

The proximity of Kentucky lent charm to my job at Karmar. On weekends, I'd take the train down to Lexington and spend Sundays moseying around the horse farms. On one of these trips I met Olin Gentry, and a friendship developed that has endured through the years. Olin was then at Colonel Edward Riley Bradley's Idle Hour Farm, where he had gone in 1921 and of which he was later manager. His brothers Charlie and Walter looked after the Idle Hour stallions. Olin welcomed my visits and encouraged me to ask questions.

Colonel Bradley was at that time the be-all and end-all of American racing, and a gambler of epic proportions. He had won the Kentucky Derby in 1921 with Behave Yourself, with his Black Servant second, but he had stood to win a fortune had the order been reversed. In 1926, the colonel was to finish one-two again in the Churchill classic with Bubbling Over and Bagenbaggage, and his Burgoo King won in 1932.

Idle Hour farm comprised about 1,800 acres along the north side of the old Frankfort Pike near Lexington, including all the land which is now Darby Dan and Danada Farms. When the colonel bought the acreage across the road that is now King Ranch, the state allowed him to construct an underpass so that his horses would not have to be led across the highway. It was at Idle Hour, on my visits with the Gentry brothers, that I resolved that some day I would be dealing solely with Thoroughbreds.

I saw my first Kentucky Derby in 1924. With an acquaintance, I left Cincinnati at 11:30 on the Friday evening before the race and we were in Louisville at 4:30 a.m. on Derby Day. We went directly to the Downs.

Dressed as I fancied a horseman of some substance should be—in derby, tweed jacket and fancy "weskit," and carrying a stick—I convinced the gate watchman that the ends of Churchill Downs would be best served by admitting me and my friend. We had our pick of grandstand seats, which were not all reserved in those days, and took turns holding our places until post time for the main event.

It was a thrilling day for me—my first Derby. I felt the quickening chill that every normal person feels when the band played "My Old Kentucky Home," and I believe I joined in for the "Weep no more, my lady" part. I was pretty well wound up by the time the horses were in a line before the starter and, like everybody else, I hollered when they left the barrier.

As I watched Black Gold make his move on the backstretch, the thought came to me that it was great to have a seat and to be able to see everything that was happening. The idea had no more than flashed through my mind when I felt a blow on the head and everything went black. Observing light when I looked down, I realized that the hysterical lady rooter behind me had buffeted me atop the bowler, ramming it down over my eyes. Black Gold swept on, while I feverishly struggled with the derby. It was no use; the fit was too tight. Finally, with the hysterical lady still pummeling, I tilted my head back and looked down my nose, thereby managing to see the final seconds of the race. It was a close finish, but I can honestly say that I saw Black Gold win the Derby.

Whenever possible I added to my library of horse books and studied and compared horses, the thing I most liked to do. Around 1922 or '23 I subscribed to *The Thoroughbred Record,* and later to *The Blood-Horse.* My father sent me *Horse and Hound* from England. I still read them all cover-to-cover weekly.

Occasionally I slipped over the river to Latonia during the race meetings there. On one of those trips I witnessed the Third International and ventured $2 on Sarazen, who ran a fantastic mile and a quarter in 2:00 ⅘ to beat Epinard. The payoff was about $13, most of which went for photos of the starters in the race, which seemed a good investment at the time. The pictures are a bit faded now, but I still have them.

The winter of 1924 was a harsh one. The Ohio River went on one of its rampages, threatening the Karmar operation. The Krippendorfs' barn was a two-story affair, and it was necessary to get the horses onto the top floor to avoid the flood. I was all alone and had a busy time moving seven horses upstairs. To complicate matters further, a freeze set in, and I was stranded there for several days.

When Karmar Stable curtailed its show activities in 1925 I changed bosses again. Mr. Woodcock gave me a wonderful testimonial letter, which I have retained and still treasure. I knew that Woodcock was completely honest, and never would recommend anyone in whom he did not have complete confidence. I believe that the years I spent under his guidance made a horseman of me.

My new job was with Julius Fleischmann of the yeast company, and my work was the care and conditioning of polo ponies and hunters. In the winter of 1924–25 Fleischmann kept twenty or thirty polo ponies and a few racehorses at Pinehurst, North Carolina. The big stable of William Ziegler, Jr., wintered there, too, under the care of W. J. Spiers; and P. S. P. Randolph also kept his racehorses at Pinehurst during the cold months.

In those days Pinehurst had a five-eighths-mile dirt track for training Thoroughbreds. Inside that was a half-mile hard-surface track for the harness horses, and that oval in turn circumscribed a steeplechase course with four or five jumps. Inside all this was a polo field. Pinehurst offered facilities for any kind of equine instruction.

Young and experimentally inclined, I rode horses of all breeds, and that winter I even rode in some races. Besides the horses owned by the well-to-do, there were a few in the neighborhood which, though legitimate representatives of the Thoroughbred breed, were not going to improve it in any way. With all this stock standing around, it was natural to hold races, so every couple of weeks we would put on an afternoon meeting. A typical program included races on the flat, some for trotters, and a steeplechase as the grand finale.

In the area was an old "gyp" owner named Kenney who had a couple of Canadian-bred geldings, Pierre Rhue and Aghamore. Both were by Glenvarloch, a stallion that had not made much of a name up to that time, and whose progeny were destined to rack up a total of $140 in earnings in 1927. Pierre Rhue and Aghamore got plenty of action on racing days. Kenney would put one in a five-eighths race and the other in a six-furlong event. Then, after the trotters had their go, both horses would perform in the steeplechase.

I made a deal with Mr. Kenney. For $250, I think it was, I bought a half-interest in the horses. Our agreement was that I would ride in suitable races, and Kenney would bear the cost of operation, which was slight. The horses were bedded down in pine needles and, for all I know, might have been fed the same thing.

Since I was too heavy to ride in the flat races, we borrowed exercise boys from someone else's stable for the running events. I rode only in the steeplechases and they were something to see. We'd go four times around on the merry-go-round that was the jumping course, which added up to a mile and a half. Then, for the exciting conclusion, the horses would duck through an opening at the head of the stretch onto the harness track, take a few steps on that hard surface, and then duck right again onto the main track for the stretch run. There was a small grandstand at the finish line. Only three or four horses would run in a steeplechase, both because the course was small and because we had only a few horses that could jump.

On one occasion I lost an iron going over the last fence. I managed to swing my horse out onto the trotting track, but in trying to swerve onto the running track I lost my balance and rolled off over the horse's withers and landed right in front of him. I was bruised and banged up some, but suffered no serious hurt. Gould Shaw, of Boston, who was at Pinehurst playing polo, administered first aid in the form of a big slug of Canadian whiskey. It was my introduction to Canadian

Club, which immediately earned a high-ranking position among my potables and a permanent place in my medicine cabinet.

Somebody drove me home to the cottage where I was staying, and I continued the treatment. I reasoned that a hot bath was the thing to round out the cure, and filled the tub. Then, as often is the case with steeplechase riders, I did a strange thing—I poured a whole bottle of Sloan's Liniment into the hot water. I lowered my aching body into the mixture and enjoyed its healing properties, but only for a short time. I soon realized that I had poured too rich a prescription. I promptly terminated the treatment, feeling looser but on fire. That might have been the only time in history that a horseman was blistered for his ills —and from the waist down. It was a harsh remedy.

The work with Fleischmann was interesting, but I had made up my mind that the Thoroughbred horse was *my* horse, and I never stopped looking for an opportunity to get into that field. So after a year with Mr. Fleischmann, I answered a help-wanted ad that Harry Rites had put in *The Thoroughbred Record.* But Rites, trainer for the Griffwood Farm, had already filled his position and had a handful of applications left, mine among them. He turned them over to another trainer, H. Guy Bedwell, who was in need of help—as always. On March 11, 1926, I received a wire from Bedwell. It said: LETTER RECEIVED COME AT ONCE GUARANTEE TERMS TO BE SATISFACTORY.

At that time, Bedwell's reputation for being a hard man (Hard Guy Bedwell, they called him) was as notorious as Father Bill Daly's had been a decade or two before. I discussed his offer with my horseman friend, W. J. Spiers, who said, "Yep, Bedwell is tough, but at least you know what you're going up against. It's your chance to get with a Thoroughbred establishment—if you can stand it."

I thought I could, and accepted. Without knowing what my salary was to be, I packed my books and my clothes and set out for Yarrow Brae, Bedwell's farm at Savage, near Laurel, Maryland. "Yarrow Brae" means "land of the free" in Gaelic, and if ever there was a misnomer, that was it. Nobody who worked for Bedwell was "free" by any stretch of the imagination. Workers were supposed to work, and he kept their noses to the grindstone day and night, seven days a week. He believed that the way to make employees do their work properly was to make them hurt if they didn't. No one stayed with him very long.

"Hard Guy" got his exercise boys and apprentice jockeys from

Canada, where he raced after the Maryland season closed in the middle of May. On his return trips from Canada, Bedwell would smuggle apprentice boys into this country. Some he hid in railroad horse cars; others rode across the bridge in the trunk of an automobile driven by a foreman or a senior rider. Some of the men brought in by Bedwell are still associated with racing in the United States.

On the farm we occasionally used whiskey for medication of foals —something of a problem due to prohibition. Bedwell had it sent from Canada, using a Pullman conductor on the Toronto-Washington express as his middleman; I'd go down to Washington and pick up the booze at Union Station. The brand was O.F.C. and when Bedwell would give me some to use on a foal, he'd say, "You can't touch this. O.F.C. means 'only for Catholics.' No Episcopalian can touch it." It was an admonition I did not follow.

A fellow over in Prince Georges County was turning out a real good Maryland rye, and he had gotten production costs down to where he could sell it for $3 a gallon. This wasn't any rotgut; it was decent drinkin' whiskey—but it wasn't as good as O.F.C. by a helluva sight. The sensible course was to reserve the Canadian whiskey for someone who would appreciate its excellent flavor, and give the good Maryland rye to the foals. The little sons of guns never noticed the difference, or at least they never complained.

Working for Bedwell was all work and no play—no stopping, no chatting, no coffee breaks, no nothing but work. Practically everyone employed there was just hanging on until he could find another job. I found another after about six months.

Nearby Laurel Park Stud was my next place of employment. That establishment was owned by a group of Englishmen who had imported the good jumpers McCarthy More and Erne; and Mount Beacon, who sired some rather good horses, among them Edith A., the dam of Riverland. Will Hayward, Jr. was the farm trainer for the stable, and I was foreman, night watchman, and general factotum. Late in 1926, Laurel Park Stud sent a draft of horses to Florida for racing. Andy Blakeley was appointed to train that division. My assignment was to take the horses south by train. The loading went smoothly until the locomotive backed up to pick up the horse car. At the time of impact, I was balanced on a partition separating two horses. The jolt projected me into the stall of a skittish three-year-old, and the crash of the couplings and my flying body did nothing to calm him down. He did a sort of tap dance on my anatomy. By the time I was dragged out, I was rather badly dented. Three ribs were fractured, my jaw was knocked out of line, and the top of my right ear was hanging by a thread of skin. The Seaboard Express waited while doctors did some fancy and effective needlework to put my ear back in place, and some elaborate taping to hold the rest of me together. When the train pulled out, I was on it.

We took the horses off at Keeney Park, later known as St. John's Park, near Jacksonville. It was a miserable experience. The food and water were so bad that the men appeased their hunger on hamburgers and quenched their thirst on soda pop. We couldn't stand the sulphur taste and odor of the water, but the horses did well on it. To top off our unhappy situation, the track didn't open, so we moved on to Miami.

In late January 1927, before Hialeah opened, I took a carload of horses back to Laurel Park for repairs. Shortly afterward the stable was disbanded. I was out of a job and out of funds, so I looked through my possessions for something hockable. Among my books was a set of *The American Turf Register* for 1829 to 1839, published by J. S. Skinner, which I had picked up for $7 sometime earlier. Suspecting that the books had some value, I shipped them to Ernest R. Gee, a New York book dealer, and promptly received a check for $100. That staggering sum of money bolstered my morale, and I was ready for almost anything, even another tour of duty with Guy Bedwell. I was hungry and H. G. was in need of a stallion man, so I was re-engaged at a fat $75 a month and board. I wasn't precisely thrilled with the idea of going back to Yarrow Brae, but I had mellowed enough to realize that if you want to learn, you have to go where the knowledge is.

The stallions Fair Gain, Thunderstorm, and Billy McLaughlin were placed in my charge. Fair Gain had been bought for $14,000 at the Saratoga sale in which Samuel D. Riddle picked up Man o' War for $5,000, but did not in the long haul prove as sound an investment.

Dr. Frank Keller was resident veterinarian at Bedwell's. I shared with him what Bedwell considered a room. It was a converted box stall situated between the apartments tenanted by Thunderstorm and Fair

Gain. One thing you had to say about Bedwell: he treated his horses as well as his people.

Doc Keller and I lived together for some time, and the association did much to advance my education. For one thing, Doc revealed to me his prescription for making bathtub gin, a valuable social asset in those days.

As all men of veterinary science know, alcohol has countless therapeutic uses. Being a vet, Doc could just about write his own ticket at the apothecary shop, which he did often enough to keep us in spirits. With the basic fluid, a drop or two of oil of juniper, a drop or two of oil of orange, and not enough water to cause rust, he could bottle a beverage that would enliven anything from a wedding to a wake. I don't know whether it was the gin, or the way we handled it, or simply nature taking its course, but we got 22 of our 23 mares in foal the spring I worked at Bedwell's with Doc Keller.

Bedwell's theories about racing were firmly grounded. He knew how to train a horse for a sprint or a route, and he knew how to bring one up to a particular race. Though irascible and demanding, he was a thorough horseman. You can learn from a man like that. You respect him for what he is, even though you can't develop an affection for him. While I sometimes questioned the wisdom of being in his employ, in later years I was amply rewarded by what I had learned in my second whirl with the "Sage of Savage." Being with Bedwell added to my store of horse lore tremendously. I gained more experience in breaking yearlings, and I learned about the horse's hoof. Few men alive knew more about feet than Bedwell, who could shoe a horse about as well as any farrier.

Things irked Guy that might not have bothered most employers. He especially didn't like his help "gallivanting around on Saturday nights." Bedwell thought a man around horses should be as fresh and alert on a Sunday morning as on a Thursday; and he took steps to see that his employees went about their tasks with their eyes open.

Respecting his knowledge of the horse's foot, I told Bedwell that if he would teach me, I would do the trimming. He agreed readily, and whenever he knew or suspected that I had crept into my quarters in the wee hours of a Sunday morning, he set me to paring hoofs. The meanest and most obstreperous cusses on the place were selected for these exercises. "I'll teach you not to run around on Saturday night," Guy would heckle, while I dodged savage teeth and hung on to a wildly swinging hoof. I didn't particularly stomach that job, but I learned how a horse's hoof is put together.

In the fall of 1927, Bedwell began to grumble about expenses. Costs were rising, he said, and the difficulties of maintaining a racing stable without going into the red were mounting. This had the earmarks of a preamble to a salary-lopping, so I bid Bedwell a final farewell.

THREE

Settling Down

After leaving Bedwell I accepted employment at Sylvester W. Labrot's Holly Beach Farm in Anne Arundel County, Maryland, where I spent ten of the happiest years of my life.

In 1910 Mr. Labrot had bought the nucleus of what grew to 2,500 acres on the Chesapeake Bay, with miles of beautiful shoreline. There he maintained a dairy herd of Jerseys as well as beef cattle. In 1926 he decided to acquire some Thoroughbreds. In England he bought thirteen mares and the stallion Sir Greysteel, a son of Roi Hérode that looked like a bigger edition of his sire. To these were added three more mares obtained in France, among them La Muiron, who was destined to produce the good and game racemare Tred Avon. Dr. John Baird, a Scotch veterinarian, had come here to run the place, and he offered me the position of managing the stallions and broodmares.

Mr. Labrot was very keen about his horses and racing, as his Frankfort, Kentucky birthplace might suggest. His vast business interests kept him occupied during his early years but, when he turned to racing and breeding, he carried with him the interest and enthusiasm that had made him a success in industry and finance. An engineer, he was head of the American Creosote Company, and was a pioneer in developing the process of treating wood, particularly railroad ties and telephone poles, with creosote. Bull pine lumber was treated under steam pressure, 500 pounds per square inch, with creosote oil. Of course, the wood lasted forever. Fences at Holly Beach made of creosoted boards held up for forty years or more.

All the Holly Beach stalls were creosoted inside every year. The wood became saturated, and half of the creosote rubbed off on the horses and blistered their hides, but that didn't worry Mr. Labrot. He held strongly to two beliefs regarding health: first that any cut, bruise, or abrasion would heal promptly if touched with a dab of creosote; and second that any illness or ailment would be cured if the patient drank Jersey milk in sufficient quantities. He may have been right about the creosote, which probably incinerated any germs that lingered in a wound, along with the adjacent hair and hide.

In 1929 he acquired additional acreage and on it built a training stable, a one-mile training track, a kitchen, and quarters for the stable help. Holly Beach expanded to the point where we had about thirty home-owned mares and about twenty-five boarders, as well as their foals and yearlings. In its ultimate development Holly Beach encompassed all the land that is now Sandy Point State Park, adjacent to the Chesapeake Bay Bridge, as well as other major holdings in the area.

During my early years at Holly Beach I attended a service at St. Margaret's Protestant Episcopal Church not far from the farm. As I glanced up from my prayer book to check the house, my eye was caught by a pretty face, and all through the years I don't think it has caught anything better. Inquiry disclosed that the face belonged to Miss Olive Macey, who lived nearby, and suddenly I found myself inspired to attend the church's Young People's Fellowship. Olive was president, and one of her duties was to make strangers feel at home. In my case, she did the job in spades.

Our first date was attended by an incident that made me realize, subconsciously perhaps, that Olive was a good person to have around. I was wearing a green-and-white striped blazer, a "baby" straw hat, white flannel trousers and black-and-white shoes. The outfit went well enough with my recently acquired Chevrolet touring car, as fine an automobile as $125 would buy. We went to a movie, then had some ice cream. It was a very pleasant evening until I tried to start the car. No luck.

The automobiles of that era were well built, but there was a standard accessory that suggested lack of confidence on the part of the manufacturer. That was the crank. If the car didn't start the way you hoped it would, you got out and turned the motor over by manpower. So I got out, took off my green-and-white blazer, carefully placed it on the clean seat, and cranked and cranked. I was dripping with perspiration, thoroughly annoyed and ruing the day I squandered the hundred and a quarter when Olive called, "Look here a minute."

I looked. "Why don't you turn this thing?" she asked.

"This thing" was the ignition key.

I turned it, stepped on the starter, and that fine, dependable car moved smoothly away. It was a rather embarrassing situation for a fellow to be in on his first date with a girl, but Olive laughed, and gave me another chance. She has been solving problems for me ever since.

One of my duties at Holly Beach was to exercise the stallion, Sir Greysteel. It didn't make any difference in which direction the big gray was ridden, so I rode him as often as not in the direction of the Maceys' place. On these exercise spins, I found myself unaccountably yearning for a glass of clear cold water, the kind that came from the Maceys' well. So while Sir Greysteel stood comfortably in the shade of the Maceys' apple tree, I sat in the kitchen and poured myself glass after glass of well water and talked to Olive. I was beginning to feel romantic.

Possibly to have time to ponder upon my future and definitely feeling the urge to see my parents and friends and my native land, I made a trip to England in 1929. It is customary for young men who have made fortunes in the New World to return home and parade their opulence before old acquaintances. I fell short on this score; my quick assets at the time I entered my father's house totaled five bucks and change. Nevertheless, the fatted calf was done in and an appropriate celebration staged, after which I borrowed shipping money from my father and embarked again for the golden land of opportunity.

I made that trip pay. My voyage to England had been on the S. S. *Minnesota*, of the Atlantic Transport Line, and I had applied for the chance to come back with some horses on one of the company's ships which sailed weekly. I was lucky. The regular man fell ill and I was given the job of taking thirty horses from London to New York. Thus I was able to cash in my return ticket, get paid by the shipping company, and arrive in America with a healthier bankroll than when I left.

For help, I had three stiffs. "Stiff" was the nautical term for an American seaman who was attending to personal business somewhere when his ship set sail from a foreign port. He immediately became the problem of the American consul, who got the man home the best way he could. The ones I drew were stiffs in every sense of the term. They didn't know anything about horses and saw no particular reason for expanding their education in that field. They did what they had to.

The best-equipped ships for horse transport had loading ramps or brows. The horses were led up these and onto the ships through a port in the side, in the area known as 'tween decks. Situated aft were about forty to fifty stalls nine or ten feet square, and there were some half-stalls as well. Usually, the better horses were put in the large boxes and the others were put in the half-stalls; it was just a question of what the shipper was willing to pay for. On this voyage I had a lot of hunters and two or three Thoroughbreds, but nothing of much consequence. Some of the horses had been bought in Ireland by American hunter dealers at the famous Dublin Horse Show.

We got into New York on a hot evening just before Labor Day. During the night the *Île de France* pulled alongside us and shut off every breath of air that might have reached us.

The *Minnesota* was not equipped with a brow, so the horses had to be slung ashore in crates. That meant putting each horse into a crate, securing him, and then slinging the crate up out of the hold and down onto the pier, where vans were waiting. Then the box was slung back to pick up another horse. The rules required that every horse be washed down from the knee and hock with a disinfectant, and that his feet be picked out and washed in the same solution. This arduous task occasionally was circumvented if the Government vet could be lured away.

We had had a big party our last night on board, so the unloading job was a punishing experience. All concerned were looking for ways to cut corners. Charlie Barry, of Teaneck, New Jersey, had nine head on the ship, and also had a load of ultra-fine Scotch under his bunk. And this was 1929, remember, when any kind of whiskey was considered drinking whiskey. Real right-off-the-boat stuff you saved only for yourself and friends, and they had to be your *very* best friends. Charlie sacrificed some of his valuable stock in the interest of expediting the unloading operation. The vet had a taste for Scotch, and was highly in favor of going where he could find some of top quality. He spent some time helping Charlie empty a bottle, greatly simplifying the proposition of getting the horses off and away and easing the anguish of my splitting head. Picking up the feet of some of those big hunters was like lifting the corner of an automobile.

Whatever pondering I had done about marriage hadn't changed anything. I still wanted to marry Olive Macey. But the lady was practical. She said, in substance, that she did not care to enter the matrimonial handicap with a champion who was carrying an impost of debt.

"Pay your father what you owe," she said. "Then we'll talk about it."

Through the munificence of the shipping company and the owners with horses on the ship, I managed this sooner than I would have believed possible, and on July 19, 1930, the strains of *Lohengrin* sounded in St. Margaret's Church. And that's the way it's been for forty-three years. We haven't made a move that wasn't completely a joint venture, and it is only thus that any success has been achieved.

We settled into a snug cottage hard by the stallion boxes at Holly Beach, and occupied ourselves with starting a family and managing a stud farm.

In 1929 Mr. Labrot had bought Happy Time, a son of High Time, and in 1932 added Blind Play, by Fair Play, Man o' War's sire. He wanted a Fair Play stallion to breed to a daughter of Sir Greysteel. He was always ready to buy a choice mare and in a few years ran his band of producers up to thirty-five.

Wise purchases and carefully planned matings resulted in the breeding of some fine runners at Holly Beach. Labrot bred Springsteel, winner of the first Maryland Futurity at Laurel, and Rush Hour, winner of the second. Springsteel, as the name suggests, was by Sir Greysteel. In addition to his Futurity success, he was the winner of the Sheridan Stakes, the Woodstock Plate and the Nassau and Miami Beach Handicaps.

Sir Greysteel also sired the superior racemare Tred Avon. In the Labrot silks that remarkable filly won the Washington Handicap at Laurel, defeating Equipoise and Mate, among others. She also racked up victories in the Arlington Matron, the Prince Georges Handicap, the King Edward Gold Cup, the Toronto Gold Cup, and the Glen Ellyn Stakes. Her full sister Monel won the New Year's and Miami Shore Handicaps.

In 1932 Mr. Labrot bought Light Brigade out of the dispersal of the stock of Senator Johnson N. Camden in Kentucky. Light Brigade, which the British Bloodstock Agency had bought for the Senator around 1915, was a big horse, sixteen hands and almost three inches, and stone blind.

I have always found it a dicey matter to move an old stallion. Most of them are slow to settle down, though Diomed, winner of the first Epsom Derby, was twenty-two years old when he came to this country, and he became a leading sire.

In my recently achieved position as stud manager, the problem of Light Brigade fell to me. We built him a special stall with a five-foot sliding door. Large vertical rollers were placed on each side of the entrance so he wouldn't injure himself going through. The stall opened onto a five-acre paddock. In Kentucky Light Brigade had been in one paddock for fifteen years before he went blind, and he knew every inch of it. Our problem was to get him familiar with his new surroundings. We led him in and out of the stall and around the paddock many times, but he was not happy in his new home.

He needed company. So I bought a donkey, which we christened Balaam. Tommy Howard, our stallion man, held Light Brigade while I led Balaam into the stall to allow the two to check each other over. There was some alfalfa in a corner, and the jackass pulled the shank right out of my hand, pushed the horse to one side, and shoved his face into the hay. In a short time the two became tremendous pals. They were a great sight, the way they played together. The old horse would nudge and push the donkey, and the donkey would back up as though he were going to kick, but he didn't.

There were times when Balaam didn't want to be bothered and would sneak away into a corner. Then Light Brigade would race around, jumping and neighing for his pal. More than one night I had to get up and help the stallion in the game of hide-and-seek. I kept a board handy and would whack old Balaam on the rump to shoo him over to where his partner was. We even hung a cowbell on him—the kind we put on cattle to keep track of them—but this donkey was cunning. When he was tired, he'd lie down and not move, the bell would be still, and Light Brigade would be puzzled.

A big gross horse, Light Brigade needed exercise, so Tommy regularly rode him around the paddock. The first day or two, Balaam would follow. Then he got smart and began cutting corners. On the third day he stood in the middle of the paddock, just like a trainer, and watched his buddy work.

We had only one small season out of Light Brigade. He died in his second season after covering just one mare, Tuckahoe, by Sir Greysteel. The resulting foal was a filly that I named Last Light; she is best remembered as the great-grandam of the fine handicap horse Vertex, sire of Kentucky Derby winner Lucky Debonair. Light Brigade was mourned and given a burial place right by the stable.

At Holly Beach we had exceptionally fine help. Seven of the men were born and reared in the area and learned their work on our farm. Tommy Howard was a superior stallion man. A Negro, he had been a jumping rider in his youth. Later, he was foreman of H. Guy Bedwell's racing stable, but had gotten fed up and asked to come with us, and I gladly took him on. The entire farm was shocked and saddened when Tommy was struck by a fatal heart attack in Sir Greysteel's stall one morning just after exercising the horse. I've often pondered on the ironic appropriateness of Tommy's passing—how a man whose life had been dedicated to horses, and who wanted no more than to be with them and serve them, lived this pattern to the last instant of his life. I think a lot of horse people live and die like this, and that they would have it no other way.

Two of our horse handlers were exceptional. Jim Inzey, our broodmare man, was huge in every dimension, the strongest man I ever saw. The horse or mare wasn't born that he couldn't handle, yet his was a firmness born of affection for the animal, and even the toughest of his charges respected him and responded to his care.

Gus Harris, a former farm teamster, was without peer as a feeder and natural nurse of a sick horse. If a horse in the racing stable was run down and not doing well, or if there was a mare or foal or yearling that wasn't thrifty, Gus could put more condition on it with less feed than anyone I ever knew. He never overfed; he just had a wonderful touch. His mares always looked exceptionally well. Doing intimate work with the individual Thoroughbred, he was second to none.

Another great old character at Holly Beach was "Dutch" Bush, who handled the farm training while Bill Irvine conditioned the horses at the track. Dutch had been with John E. Madden at Hamburg Place for a long period of time. Later he was superintendent of B. B. Jones's Audley Farm at Berryville, Virginia, and at William Ziegler, Jr.'s Burrland Farm at Middleburg. From Dutch, I received a real education in the care of breeding stock, and learned extensively of Mr. Madden's very successful methods of racehorse production.

The Labrot horses raced on all fronts—Canada, Detroit, New Orleans, Kentucky, Florida, New York, and of course Maryland. Besides Springsteel and Tred Avon, we had dozens of other winners, including Stainforth, who won the Aberdeen Stakes, and Toolbox, a favorite of mine. But fortune did not always smile. In fact, there was a series of disasters that might have run anyone but a thorough sportsman right out of the game.

In 1933 Holly Beach Farm, like a good many other farms in southern Maryland and up the Jersey coast, was struck by an epidemic of sleeping sickness—equine encephalomyelitis. It took two forms: some of the horses simply stood in a corner with their heads hanging down until they died, sleeping themselves to death; others went crazy and had to be shot quickly. I carried a Colt .45 and a box of shells in my car at all times, and too often I had to use the gun. We lost the dam of Tred Avon, the dam of Toolsteel, a good Fair Play mare and several of our best yearlings and fillies that were not yet in training.

Though nothing was known about the disease in the East, there had been a dreadful outbreak in the San Joaquin Valley in California.

The Cutter Laboratory had developed a serum which was the only known preventative. We spent $1,500 for some of this West Coast serum, but it proved to be ineffective in treating the Eastern strain of the virus. Later research revealed that the infection was transmitted by salt marsh mosquitoes. After drawing the blood of an ailing animal, the insects carried the infection to others on which they fed. When we found what the causative agent was, we sprayed everything with insecticide.

I had been advised to keep the horses in and not out in the field where they would have been prey to the mosquitoes, and this saved some of them. But the epizootic at Holly Beach lasted from August to October. In that time forty-four horses, ponies, hacks, and mules were infected, of which twenty-two died or had to be destroyed. For years Mr. Labrot had insured all his stock for full mortality but, about 1930, he decided to "self-insure" his animals. Every horse lost to encephalomyelitis was a dead loss. After the scourge, I wrote a complete report of our experience for Cutter Laboratory, giving a detailed case history of every horse involved.

To add to Labrot's misfortunes, Springsteel broke a shoulder racing at Rockingham Park. He was buried in the centerfield there. Monel broke down, and King's Pleasure, Stainforth, and Blast Furnace also were rendered *hors de combat.* Then came a real crusher. Toolbox, Little Dinah, and King's Pleasure finished first, third, and fourth, as listed, in the Maryland Futurity of 1934, with Toolbox ten lengths ahead at the wire. A foul by one of the lesser lights of the entry resulted in a disqualification, and in those days, the stewards didn't try to pick out the one to blame. When an entry was disqualified, every horse in it was set back.

Shortly afterward, Toolbox was cut down in the Walden at Pimlico and went on the injured-reserved list. Trainer Jim Ryan acquired him after Mr. Labrot's death and the gray became a topflight jumper in the stable of General Richard K. Mellon.

All three of our children were born at Holly Beach. Patricia Jane arrived on April 26, 1931, Laura Marguerite Stanley on November 24, 1932, and John Michael Stanley on June 4, 1934.

We never had much in the way of money on the farm. I had my

pay cut twice the first year of my marriage—it was the Depression and everybody's pay was being cut. But we didn't lack for food; we had all the milk we could drink, plenty of vegetables, and oysters, crabs, and fish right out of the Chesapeake Bay.

And living in Maryland offered plenty in the way of both occupation and diversion to a horseman and his family. For many years the Maryland Hunt Cup, run in late April, was picnic time for the Finneys. When the children were young, we used to pack lunch and drive up from Holly Beach for a day's outing on the greensward of Worthington Valley. People would come from hundreds of miles away to witness the colorful and exciting event, staged against a spectacularly beautiful background. Pennsylvanians and Virginians of the hunt and polo set would show up with their station wagons loaded with provender and revitalizing liquids. In the old days, for which many of us feel nostalgia, bookmakers set up their row of slates, adding to the sporting aspect of the race. The prices were always points short of what they should have been, but most people bet only a dollar or two, just for fun.

No ordinary horse can go the tough four-mile course of the Maryland, much less win it, and no rider with a trace of chicken in his make-up can go the twenty-two fences. It is a race for brave men and bold horses. Among the fine horses I saw take the Hunt Cup was Blockade, winner in three consecutive years, from 1938 to 1940. Another three-time winner was Winton, owned, trained and ridden by Stuart S. Janney, Jr., one of the best riders I ever saw in the race. I remember well Mrs. Marion du Pont Scott's brilliant Trouble Maker, who won in 1932 and died after a bone-shattering fall at the seventeenth fence in 1935. Noel Laing, his rider, knelt beside him, overcome by sorrow. Trouble Maker was buried near the spot where he fell.

I didn't miss many Hunt Cups while I was based in Maryland, and made it back whenever I could after I had moved to other places. And in 1947, the year of Winton's second victory, I assumed the difficult task of broadcasting the running of the Cup. The setup was sensationally different from what it is today, when great sports events are presented on television and the scene of action crawls with producers, directors, and technicians. Then, a fellow handed me a microphone and said, "Start talking."

Visibility was poor, and my task was made more complex by a

youngster who was watching the race from a tree above my head. His moves, in following the race, caused a branch to whack me in the face as I attempted to broadcast.

"John," I called to my son who was assisting me, "get that kid out of the tree!"

John's response was not helpful.

"Pa," he said, "I'm afraid you can't do much about that kid. His father owns the place."

The Maryland Hunt Cup has been a source of great enjoyment for my family and me. The pleasant afternoons, the hot days, the too-cold-for-comfort ones and the blinding rainstorms—all were part of the Cup and the adventures that went with it. As Bryce Wing, secretary, once told an inquiring reporter when the weather was particularly vile, "The Maryland Hunt Cup is never postponed."

In the Maryland years I continued my association with horse shows, a connection that began in my childhood in England when I showed a Shire broodmare for a Cheshire farmer during my holidays from school. In Maryland I became interested in hunter, equitation, and breeding classes. In the mid-twenties I exhibited horses in breeding shows in Maryland and elsewhere. We took yearlings from Holly Beach down to Upperville, Virginia, where the finest young Thoroughbred stock was exhibited.

I started judging while I was still at Holly Beach. Later, when I was field secretary of the Maryland Horse Breeders Association, judging shows in the state or out of it became a regular Saturday occupation. The American Horse Shows Association, which rates judges as seniors or juniors depending on their experience, rated me a senior in draft, breeding, hunter, jumper, equitation and polo classes. I always kept myself a junior in the saddle and walking horse divisions, as I did not enjoy judging them, so never bothered to achieve senior status.

I served on several occasions at the National Horse Show in Madison Square Garden, where I once had the responsibility of judging both the hunter and saddle-seat equitation classes. That year both divisions were won by the same young lady, Miss Barbara Pease, later well known in the Thoroughbred world as Mrs. L. Clay Camp of Glenmore Farm, Charlottesville, Virginia. Not many riders have performed the feat of scoring such a double.

I have judged at the Royal Winter Fair in Toronto and at the International Livestock Exhibition in the Chicago stockyards. But the shows at Upperville, where in 1970 I judged for the fourth time in thirty-five years, were the best of all. Generally speaking, the breeding classes of the late sixties were not what they were a few decades earlier, because it's not easy to get breeders to exhibit their horses. There never is enough help on the farms, and the farm hands are by no means show-minded. Thirty years ago, there was a great rivalry among the grooms of northern Virginia for blue ribbons and championships in the breeding classes at Upperville, Culpeper, Orange, and Warrenton.

I always took a deep interest in the development of ponies and in encouraging children to ride. Children, like two-year-old racehorses, generally give their best. They haven't gotten sharp and cunning like some older riders. When they've made a mistake they usually listen to a word of correction with better grace than their elders.

Once after I had judged a pony show I received a telephone call from the father of one of the exhibitors, and not a first-prize winner. When you place a horse or pony first and get a call from an interested party, you feel relaxed; but when it's from the parent of a loser, you have to be on your guard.

This call was different; the father was laughing. "When Ronnie got home," he said, "I asked him how he made out. He said, 'All right, I guess, Pop. I got a red ribbon.' And then he added, 'But if Mr. Finney had looked through those glasses instead of over them, I'd have won the blue.' "

A long time ago I judged a show on the Eastern Shore of Maryland. It was a real "country" show where I had to do just about everything. After I had designated the conformation and performance winners, I was named starter and sole judge for several races for local horses to be run over a roughly oval course laid out in a large meadow. These events, I soon learned, were run under Marquis of Queensberry Rules, rather than those of the National Steeplechase and Hunt Association.

In the opening race a rider, who subsequently reached the finish line first, deliberately shut off another, forcing his victim to pull up sharply or plow into the spectators. As I was judge, jury, steward and high Pooh-Bah, I immediately disqualified the bounder. It was one of the bigger mistakes of my life, and I've made my share.

The male members of the rough rider's family were legion in number, brawny of conformation and fluent in their indignation. In the morning horse show they had won a large trophy, which they kept filled with local moonshine. Their spokesmen, of which there were several, described the disqualification as unfair and uncalled for, as even a blind man could see that it was the other guy's fault; and what did I expect their boy to do, let the other fellow through? One particularly belligerent individual made it clear that he hadn't said his whole piece, as I would jolly well find out after the last race.

Right there, on the spur of the moment, I decided to forego the pleasure of witnessing the last event. I sent off the next one, slipped away during the excitement of the contest and started a race of my own for the Annapolis ferry. I don't know who finished in the place and show spots, as I was safely out in the Chesapeake Bay before the lynching party, if there was one, reached the dock.

Judging is a ticklish job. It requires a thorough knowledge of conformation and of what to expect in performance, and that comes only through observation, experience and careful study. Besides, a judge must have absolute confidence in his own ability and be ready to defend his opinions, for there'll be times when he'll have to.

If a judge is a knowledgeable man, fair and on the level, as ninety-nine percent of them are, he won't mind answering questions if they're put to him in the right way. I'm not talking about the few stuffed shirts who are out there only because of social position or national prominence; I mean the true, down-to-earth horsemen who can take an animal apart muscle by muscle and bone by bone. Many of our socialites and celebrities qualify handsomely, but because of their knowledge, *not* because of their positions.

The judge that I consider the right kind is the man or woman who has complete confidence in his knowledge and is willing to share it. If your horse finishes second or third or farther back, such an official generally will tell you why he put other horses ahead of yours. He might say "I didn't think your horse was as good a mover as the winner," or "He didn't stride out as well," or "I don't think your horse had as good a hind leg, and I'm a bug on a straight hind leg." Generally, if you put your questions to the judge politely, you'll get a satisfactory answer.

Sylvester W. Labrot died in New Orleans of a cerebral hemorrhage on February 22, 1935, at the age of sixty-three. The atmosphere at Holly Beach was steeped in sorrow. Mr. Labrot was buried on the farm on a knoll overlooking Meredith Creek and Whitehall Bay, not far from the Chesapeake. He deeply loved his beautiful Holly Beach, and it was fitting that he should rest there. I can't describe the personal loss I felt.

Mrs. Labrot carried on with the stud after her husband died. A very charming lady, a native of New Orleans, she was a great-granddaughter of James Jackson, who had imported Galopade, the great foundation mare, whose name is found in the pedigrees of many horses. Jackson also imported Glencoe, a Two Thousand Guineas winner, and Lapdog and St. Giles, winners of the Epsom Derby. Glencoe, of course, had an excellent career, and his daughters were much sought after as broodmares. The two Derby winners didn't do much.

I got Mrs. Labrot interested in producing a history of the development of the Thoroughbred through James Jackson's importations. We accumulated a fine file of material and I was working toward publication when Mrs. Labrot died, three years after her husband, and the project was abandoned. The high days of Holly Beach Farm were gone forever.

FOUR

Branching Out

I was elected to the board of directors of the Maryland Horse Breeders Association in 1936.

Since at Holly Beach I was intimately associated with horses and their problems I found myself with the urge to write about them, and Mr. Labrot had encouraged me. To my surprise and delight *The Thoroughbred Record* accepted my first effort, which if memory serves was a brief piece about King George V and his interest in the Royal stud at Sandringham. Better still, the editor of the *Record* invited me to send along more material, and the first thing I knew, I was a "turf journalist." Perhaps my most ambitious project up to this time was "A Stud Farm Diary," a day-by-day account of my life and work as manager at Holly Beach, published as a serial by *The Blood-Horse* during 1935–36 and first published in book form by that magazine in December 1936.

So at my first board meeting of the Maryland Horse Breeders Association, it was natural that I should propose that the Association regularly publish a mimeographed bulletin to keep the members and interested outsiders informed about what was going on. The other directors approved the idea, and I was appointed a committee of one to put out the sheet.

Charlie Williams, a long-time Maryland breeder, thought *The Maryland Horse* would be a good name. The first issue appeared in July 1936. It was a four-page printed folder; when we got right down to it, we felt mimeographing wasn't quite good enough.

Shortly after the folder had been distributed, a live-wire printer presented the directors with a plan for a more pretentious publication. So the September 1936 issue consisted of eight pages, and the cover illustration was a picture of Canter, the first Maryland-bred horse to win over $150,000.

Working full time at Labrot's and almost full time for the Maryland Horse Breeders, I found myself nearly swamped under labors of my own creation. About that time, a group of Virginia breeders decided to reorganize a moribund association and called on me for assistance and recommendations. I spent some time with them, explaining the pattern that had been used in organizing the Maryland association; as a result of my visit, the Virginia breeders made me an offer. I never had hesitated to jump from one job to another when I felt it was the right thing to do, but I had formed a strong attachment to Maryland and was not anxious to move. My problem was solved for me in 1937 when twenty Maryland breeders subscribed to a fund to underwrite *The Maryland Horse* and guarantee me an annual salary as editor and field secretary of the Association. I really hated to leave Holly Beach Farm, but the magazine and the work for the Association presented an appealing challenge, and I felt that there might be even broader horizons ahead.

My admiration and regard for Chester Hockley, who had been elected president of the Association in 1936, influenced me to some extent. As president, Hockley set about putting life into the organization, and during his administration it developed in a healthy manner. A broader system of registration was instituted and breeders' sales became a part of the annual routine. I was given an open charter to do anything I saw fit to further the interests of horse breeding in Maryland. Moving around the state, I spent much time with young folk, encouraging and instructing them whenever possible, as I felt the future of the horse industry depended on them.

As field secretary I thought my headquarters should be centrally situated, so I moved my family first to a cottage on Highland Avenue in Towson, then around the corner to One Dixie Drive, which also became the address of *The Maryland Horse* and of the Association.

To me, One Dixie Drive will always be a place of fond memories. While I was there, *The Maryland Horse* grew, the Maryland Horse Breeders Association developed into an organization of some influence in the community, and I grew, too. I was able to follow my urge to get into new things like shows, fairs, and sales—particularly sales.

I made a number of trips to Saratoga and to the Lexington sales before I became officially attached to a sales company. I bought my first horse at Saratoga for Mr. Labrot in 1927: Dinah Did, by Upset out of Dinah Do, by Colin; two years later she won the Test Stakes.

I started announcing Thoroughbred auctions for the Fasig-Tipton Company at Pimlico in 1937. At that sale C. V. Whitney sold his racing stable, including Dauber, the 1938 Preakness winner, who brought $40,000.

In the fall of 1941 the Maryland Horse Breeders Association put on a sale for Leslie E. Keiffer, of Inverness Farm, Monkton. Mr. Keiffer was on the Cotton Exchange, and his major client was the Japanese government. As might be expected in that year, his business suffered somewhat, so he decided to sell his horses. He had two stallions, Jean Bart and Charing Cross, about twenty mares, a dozen or more yearlings and about the same number of weanlings.

Jean Bart had been a moderate kind of racehorse. He had raced for Walter M. Jeffords, and was acquired by Keiffer in a transaction engineered by Neil Newman, a turf journalist and part-time horse trader. Jean Bart's pedigree could not be faulted: he was by Man o'War out of Escuina, by Ecouen, and therefore was a full brother to the great race-mare Bateau. Like many other outstanding runners of the day, he had a double infusion of Fairy Gold. But despite his bloodlines, the horse had little appeal. His first two-year-olds had raced in '41 and had done little to send breeders rushing to their sire.

Charing Cross, by Sir Gallahad III out of Cross of Gold, by Gay

Crusader, belonged to Keiffer and Marshall Field, and was being sold to dissolve the partnership. Charing Cross had a bit of promise, but Keiffer didn't think much of him.

All the yearlings and weanlings were by Jean Bart, and all but two of the pregnant mares were in foal to the same sire, so if a person didn't fancy Jean Bart, there wasn't much to interest him in Keiffer's stock. Keiffer asked me for suggestions, and I recommended that he hold the sale between the Havre de Grace and Laurel meetings in late September. Havre closed September 27, and Laurel didn't open until October 1. (The frantic governmental urge to exploit every possible racing day did not come until years later.)

I also suggested that Keiffer put on a real good lunch with plenty to eat and drink, and have it at his lovely old colonial home at Inverness. "Entertain everybody," I said, "and don't forget the grooms and van men. See that they have beer and food. Often buyers ask them questions and you want them on your side."

Shortly after this, I met the local liquor dealer. "What in the world is Mr. Keiffer up to?" he asked. "I've had the damnedest order for whiskey, beer, and champagne from him."

"Mr. Keiffer's going to have a good sale," I explained. "That's what he's up to."

The day of the sale was extremely cold, much colder than usual for that time of year, and a real sharp wind was blowing. People came —not too many of them—and were steered into the house for the presale warmup. A chap who had silk and lace mills in New England was on hand with a lady friend who fancied herself a judge of Thoroughbred conformation and pedigree, and to whose opinion the silk man deferred on all his selections. Billy Vaughan of Red Bank, New Jersey, was there with Mrs. Vaughan. So was G. Ray Bryson, of Kingsville, Maryland. There were some others but, I thought, not *enough* others. When I went into the box with George Swinebroad before the sale, I could count only 102 people, and some of them I knew weren't going to buy anything.

But Keiffer had put alcohol into them and then stuffed them with turkey, scrambled eggs, sausages, ham, and hot biscuits—everything to give a person that contented, prosperous feeling on a cold day. When the sale started at two o'clock, everybody was ushered out to the sales ring and the house was locked up. No one was allowed in until the sale was over.

Charlie Howard, of Seabiscuit fame, had called me that morning from California. He was interested in a half sister to a very good horse he owned, and wanted to know what I thought of the sale.

"I don't think anything is going to bring much money," I told him. "It looks to me that you'll be able to buy anything you want at your own price."

"What do you think this mare will bring?" he asked.

"Oh," I said, "about $2,500 or $3,000."

"Well," he said, "go to about $4,000, if you have to."

"You'll get her for that," I assured him.

Well sir, in view of the stock offered, I never saw a better sale. Keiffer's hospitality had put a charm over the gathering. The atmosphere was friendly, cordial, and informal, and we dealt with the buyers in a conversational manner.

"Now, Mr. Bryson," I would say, "you're not going to let Mr. Vaughan take this away from you—this lovely mare—at that sort of a price. I know it isn't anything like her value." When the New England silk man was interested in a horse, he'd edge forward, and I'd address the girl friend: "Miss So-and-so, I'm sure you know the value of this animal. It's much more than the amount being offered. It's the sort of thing Mr. So-and-so should have."

By playing one buyer against another, with everybody relaxed, we sold horses as though they weren't being manufactured any more. Neil Newman was running a tab in his catalogue and every once in a while he'd put down the book and rub his hands in glee. I was astounded. Nobody wanted the Jean Barts, but they bought them anyway—thanks to Keiffer's hospitality.

After the sale, Keiffer broke out the champagne and we celebrated. In the middle of that joyous session, Charlie Howard called and asked if I had gotten the mare for him.

"No," I replied. "She brought $9,000."

"Well, why didn't you buy her?"

"You only told me to go to $4,000."

"I'd have given a lot more," Howard said, "but you thought $4,000 would get her."

"I did," I admitted, "but I was wrong."

That sale grossed three times as much as we'd expected. Sad to relate, however, none of the horses did very much except the stallion Charing Cross, who was bought by Lawrence Sheppard of the Hanover Shoe Farm in Pennsylvania, one of the world's greatest trotting horse nurseries. Mr. Sheppard was interested in having a few Thoroughbred mares on the place for his daughter, and wanted a stallion. Charing Cross got quite a number of winners—many that were good, useful performers on the half-mile ovals. But Jean Bart never lived up to his pedigree.

When World War II broke out, I was still an English citizen, so I offered my services to Britain. I was rejected, but I found a war job in America instead.

Early in the war, while German submarines were cruising up and down the Atlantic Coast, it was feared that spies and saboteurs might be landed from the submarines on remote beaches. To cork up this loophole, the Coast Guard Beach Patrol was formed, and I was called in to help with the planning and with the procurement of animals. The Maryland Horse Breeders Association granted me a wartime leave of absence so I could devote full time to government service.

The original idea, during the early periods of hysteria, was to get private owners to loan their riding horses. I felt it would be better to use Remount horses, and this suggestion was followed. Starting in the summer of 1942, we eventually put 5,000 horses on the beaches, wherever the terrain permitted their use.

I was sent to the Seventh Naval District in Florida to work with the Beach Patrol, and was given the title of Associate Technologist and Assistant to the Commandant. Since I was not an American citizen I could not be given a commission, but I received a lieutenant commander's pay and didn't have to salute anybody, even an admiral, and I could act without having to unwind the red tape.

Few of the enlisted men had had any experience with horses, and many were a little scared about working with them. Some were petrified, though they tried not to show it. Actually, it was easier to train the horses than the men. The animals were used to having people around them, whereas the adventure was a completely new experience to the men. Nevertheless, in less time than I would have believed possible, we had most of the young men handling their mounts in a satisfactory manner, and some of them became really decent horsemen.

We were supplied with McClellan saddles, which the Army had been using since the Civil War, I think, with only slight modifications —flaps and current-model stirrups. Men who had had riding experience tried to adapt the McClellan to their styles. The racetrack lads— former exercise boys and ex-jockeys—shortened the stirrup straps; the Western riders lengthened them. But before long, the cowboys were shortening their stirrup straps and the jockeys were letting them out, because there's only one way to sit a McClellan saddle, and that's the way the Army intended—about halfway between the normal hunting seat and the cowboy seat. A rider can't adapt the McClellan to *his* style; he has to change his style to fit the saddle.

The horses were especially useful at night, since they could see and sense things that could not be picked up by the duller faculties of human beings. If anything was amiss, the horse usually saw it first and signaled by shying or pricking up his ears. It was the duty of the rider to call out a challenge when something aroused his suspicions. At first the men felt silly, crying out a challenge in the vast emptiness of night, sky, sea and sand, but they soon found that the horse's sense was infallible, and if a horse said that danger was near, it was time to investigate.

Later in the war, when radar stations had been installed along the beaches, the Beach Patrol was shelved, leaving the Coast Guard with several thousand horses. The Army Remount Service had also outlived its usefulness, with the "cavalry" now operating on gasoline and diesel oil instead of oats. So when I returned from annual leave late in the summer of 1943, I was handed the assignment to "get rid of the horses" for the Coast Guard and the Remount Service.

Working for the Surplus Property Section of the Procurement Division of the Treasury, I spent thirteen months in 1943 and 1944 traveling and holding sales. I traveled the coastline from Asbury Park, New Jersey, to Brownsville, Texas, and from the Mexican border to Vancouver, British Columbia, going by plane, train, boat, jeep, truck, automobile and on horseback. There were days when we sold as many as four or five hundred horses.

On two days in March 1944, Captain Harry Hayman and I sold 505 horses at the stockyards south of San Francisco. I rode a horse around the big square corral and used a megaphone to do the announcing. When the second day of selling was over, Captain Hayman and I felt well pleased with the results, so, before starting for our next stop at San Mateo, we put away a few drinks—some to take off the chill, for it had been a cold, raw day, and some just for sociability.

Rolling down El Camino Real, with a feeling of warmth toward all mankind and the conviction that all was right with the world, we came upon an unusual sight. In the slow lane, a car was traveling much more slowly than the recommended speed. A lady was driving, and the back seat was loaded with kids. A man's arm was thrust out the right front window, and attached to the man's arm was a horse!

Clear of mind as we were, we recognized at once that the horse was one we had auctioned off just a short time earlier. "That's an old gentleman who came up to talk to me during the sale," I said to Captain Hayman. "He's an old cavalry officer and he wanted to buy a horse for his grandchildren."

In our amiable frame of mind, we decided to be helpful. Pulling our car off the road, we signaled for the lady to pull in behind us.

I went back and asked, "Are you having a bit of trouble, Colonel?"

"Well," he answered, "the trip has been more difficult than I expected." He introduced the lady as his daughter-in-law and the minors as his grandchildren.

I felt even more amiable.

"Hayman," I called, "we have a saddle and bridle in the car. Throw 'em on this animal and I'll ride him."

"Oh no," the lady said, "we couldn't put you out that way."

I assured them that it was nothing, and mounted the horse. The colonel drove one car and the captain another and I trotted along down El Camino Real about twenty miles, with cars roaring past at sixty miles an hour. It was a lot of fun for all, and I demonstrated that that horse was a fitting mount for a small child or an idiot.

The Los Angeles sale was glamorized by a slight touch of Hollywood: movie actresses helped show the horses before the selling.

One extremely presentable equine attracted a number of bids. Its service record showed that it was gentle, and a safe animal for a child. A proud Los Angeles father bought it for his offspring, a boy about fourteen years old, who was present and egging his parent on. The lad was dressed in full cowboy regalia, from expensive white Stetson to spurs that jangled when he walked. When the horse passed into his possession, he dragged out a handsome Mexican saddle which he and his pappy slung over the horse's withers. Then they shoved the animal's face through a bridle that dripped with tinkling silver ornaments and was furnished with a spade bit.

The horse chewed suspiciously at the bit and got a funny look in his eye. The youthful Lone Ranger sprang lightly into the saddle, accompanied by the music of his spurs and other noisy accoutrements, but before you could say Tonto he was describing a graceful arc through the California ozone. A conveniently-situated manure pile cushioned his fall, but did not prevent serious damage to his dignity.

The father was on top of me in a second, wanting to know what the hell was the idea of representing a half-broken rodeo bronco as a suitable mount for a child. I explained that the horse was a creature of simple tastes, and that under the equipment the Cavalry had put on him he had always behaved like a gentleman. I couldn't help adding that the assortment of noisy dinguses they had draped over him was enough to scare him out of his wits.

That sale was voided and the horse was resold—at a higher price.

At High Island, Texas, the Beach Patrol had had a horse that was a real mean rascal; nobody could do a thing with him. Then along came a lad who gentled the horse, broke him, and finally made a decent riding horse of him.

When this horse came up for sale, the boy who had managed him wanted him badly, and asked his father to buy him. I was announcing, and I told the story when the animal was led into the ring, hoping the horse would end up with the boy who had devoted so much time to it.

The father started bidding. Everybody there was rooting for him to get the horse. But also on hand was an Eastern horse dealer, who was buying one horse at a time; when he'd get a carload, he'd ship 'em away. Everyone watched to see if he'd put a bid on the boy's pet horse.

Sure enough, he did. A groan was heard, because everyone felt he could certainly outbid the boy's father. But the old gent bumped the bid up a notch and was high man again.

Before the dealer could open his mouth, he found himself looking up at a huge Texan, great big hat and all, and he suddenly realized that every eye in the place was on him.

The Texan looked the dealer up and down for a minute and then inquired, "Were you bidding on this horse?"

"Oh, no. No. I wasn't bidding on the horse," the man assured him.

"I didn't think you were," the Texan said, and turned away.

At that moment somebody hollered, "Sold!" and the horse was on the way home, destined to spend the rest of his life with the youngster who had made a useful animal of him.

At one sale, almost every horse brought forward was afflicted with splints, ringbones or sidebones. Some of the animals were bought by people who were not exactly knowledgeable horsefolk and didn't realize that these were defects. Between sellings, a lady came up to me and said, "I've been trying all afternoon to get one of those ringbone horses, and somebody always overbids me."

"Lady, I have a pleasant surprise for you," I said. "The next one coming up has *two* ringbones."

The lady bid eagerly, and went away completely happy—the owner of a double ringbone horse!

By the time the last government horse had gone under the hammer, I had traveled 60,000 miles and had inspected and sold 24,000 horses. The bottom price was $25, the top $675, and the average $75. It was my contribution to the war effort; it was fun; and it was useful experience—how useful I was soon to realize, as I became more and more involved in arranging and conducting horse sales of a very different kind.

FIVE

The Siren Song: Fasig-Tipton

William B. Fasig, short, dapper, and ambitious, was secretary of the Cleveland Driving Club in the early 1890s. He loved luxury and, to provide himself with the better things in life, he got backing from men of substance and started organizing sales of horses, mostly trotters, which he staged in a king-size sales arena he had constructed across from the Driving Club Park. His success attracted the attention of Tattersalls, the famous English horse-trading company, who invited him to set up trotting sales for them in New York, with branches in Chicago, Cleveland, San Francisco and Lexington, Kentucky.

Fasig accepted, and took Enoch James Tranter along with him. Tranter, who had been stable boy, office assistant and man of all work, was a young Englishman who had immigrated to Cleveland.

After a short period of prosperity, the panic of 1893 turned the horse business sour. Tattersalls panicked along with nearly everyone else, and unloaded their American interests on Fasig.

In 1898 he took Ed A. Tipton as a partner and the Fasig-Tipton

44

Company was formed. The company sold high-class road and driving horses, and all kinds of carriages and coaches. They also sold racing stock, both Thoroughbred and Standardbred, although in those days the emphasis was on Standardbreds. Their offices at that time were in the original Madison Square Garden. At Fasig's death in 1903, Tipton assumed control of the company, with Tranter as his chief assistant.

The company's principal sale, held every December, was called the Old Glory sale. After the Old Glory sale of 1907, disaster struck. Financial panic swept New York and the Knickerbocker Trust closed holding all the consignors' money. That was enough for Tipton. He told Tranter that if he could get the consignors paid off, the business was his.

Tranter had plenty of guts. He was a rough character and a tough man to deal with when he wanted to be. Instead of giving up hope, he went to another bank that was headed by a man who was prominent in harness racing and a Fasig-Tipton client. The banker assured Tranter that the panic would pass, that the Knickerbocker Trust would reopen, and that the money was safe. To emphasize his optimism, he advanced Tranter sufficient funds to pay off all debts to consignors and to carry on the business.

Tranter ran the company efficiently, holding sales at Durland's Riding Academy, Madison Square Garden, the tracks at Sheepshead Bay and Belmont and other places. He changed the format of the sales catalogue. Instead of listing thirty dams back to Old Bald Peg, he stressed what closer relatives had done in performance and production. He was also the first to insist on certificates of health and pregnancy in broodmare sales.

On the advice of William Woodward, Sr., Arthur B. Hancock, Sr., Hal Price Headley and others, the Kentucky breeders who had been selling their yearlings in New York gave Tranter their backing. He purchased land and built the sales setup at Saratoga, and the custom of selling yearlings during the race meeting there was inaugurated under Tranter's management in 1917.

Tranter died in 1939. His widow, Mrs. Katherine I. Tranter, continued the business with the aid of Ed Shields, secretary, and Dave Morenberg, bookkeeper.

During World War II breeders were not permitted to ship their yearlings freely around the country, so Saratoga was abandoned after the 1942 sale, not to reopen until 1946. Fasig-Tipton held the 1943 sale in a tent at the Keeneland Racecourse in Lexington. It was at this sale that Fred W. Hooper, Jr. bought Hoop Jr., his first racehorse, for $10,200. He won the 1945 Kentucky Derby with the colt.

The Kentucky breeders asked Fasig-Tipton to spend one per cent of their five per cent income from the sale on advertising, because they feared that buyers would not come to Lexington. Mrs. Tranter and Shields refused, with the result that the men who had backed Tranter in 1917 formed a breeders' cooperative and held their own sale. From this came the Keeneland Sales Company—a thorn in the flesh of the old organization.

I had started going to Saratoga in the twenties. I'd stay in Sunny Jim Fitzsimmons's stable area. Mr. Fitz was very good to me, as he always was to interested youngsters; and while at that time I may not have been so young, I was certainly interested.

At Saratoga I became very friendly with some men who worked for Fasig-Tipton and also with old man Tranter. In those days he had a virtual monopoly in the sales business and could get away with almost anything. He believed that the customer was *never* right, regardless of whether the customer in question was buyer or seller. I remember in 1929 when the Eastland Farms syndicate paid $75,000 for New Broom and Tranter said, "Ladies and gentlemen, *no* yearling is worth $75,-000!" He was right in that case, at least—New Broom was utterly useless. The horse wound up as a mount for Captain Leslie White, referee of the polo matches of the Meadowbrook Club.

Tranter was very friendly to me. First of all, I was an English immigrant, like him. But the main thing was that I was always around and available. My work with the Maryland Horse Breeders gave me leeway to do anything that didn't interfere with my duties in Maryland, so I spent a good deal of time at the sales, watching what was going on.

I was especially interested in the auction announcer. I always thought the announcer would do a better job if he didn't just sit there beside the auctioneer with his head down, gabbling out of a book, but acted as if he were really in charge and knew the value of the animals that were being sold. All my working life had been spent with the horse himself, and I felt I knew the value of a horse and could get the point across to the customers. Announcing was a job I thought I could do, and do well.

As I've mentioned, I announced for Fasig-Tipton for the first time at the Whitney sale in 1937. I still have the letter Tranter wrote me telling me what good work I had done in the stand. After Tranter died, however, his job as announcer was given to Brownie Leach, a Kentuckian, because, so I was told, they wanted a soft Kentucky drawl coming from the stand. But I continued announcing at the breeders' sales in Maryland, and I kept on going to the Saratoga sales until the war closed Saratoga in 1942.

In 1943, Mrs. Tranter offered to sell me the business and good will of the Fasig-Tipton Company for $30,000. At that time I was up to my ears in Coast Guard work and didn't want to quit until the job was done; but I told Ray Bryson and Henry Knight, then vice-president of the trucking division of General Motors, about the offer. They agreed to put up the money and cut me in for a third to run the business when I was released from my government duties. I offered half my share— a sixth of the company—to Ed Shields, asking him just to sit in the New York office and keep things going until I got out; but he wasn't interested. So that ended that. Mrs. Tranter held the company for another two years and then sold out to Major Kenneth N. Gilpin and W. H. LaBoyteaux. Major Gilpin, a former Air Force officer, was a breeder who among other things had imported the successful French stallion Teddy, sire of Sir Gallahad III and Bull Dog, to Virginia. He retained me as an adviser and sales assistant—responsibilities I added to the various posts I already held in Maryland.

Major Gilpin died in 1947 and was succeeded as president of Fasig-Tipton by his son, Tyson. In 1950 I was made a vice-president of the company and also became a stockholder. Then, in 1952, Tyson Gilpin announced that he and his family would sell a sizable portion of their Fasig-Tipton stock and that he would step down as president, for he wanted to have more time for his family and his Kentmere Farm at Boyce, Virginia. The Gilpins retained some of their holdings, but wished to make shares in the company available to Thoroughbred breeders who were regular consignors to the Saratoga sales and to other interested people we wanted in. I was given the post of executive vice-president and general manager and the opportunity to reorganize the company.

I recognized at once that I would have to give up my Maryland duties at last and that, moreover, some time would be required for me to find others to take over my Maryland work. So I asked for a year to conclude my affairs in the Free State. As things turned out, however, my most important problems were solved more quickly than I had believed possible. Stewart Sears, my valued associate for many years, took over the management of the Maryland Horse Breeders Association, and Raleigh Burroughs, editor of *Turf and Sport Digest*, assumed the responsibility of putting out *The Maryland Horse*. Early in 1953, with my Maryland affairs in order, I was ready to leave, and my friends gave me a going-away party. The racing writers and horse breeders collaborated in a sendoff that Olive and I will remember and cherish to the end of our days.

With considerable sadness of heart, I abandoned the brick cottage at One Dixie Drive, Towson, and found a place in Rye, New York, within commuting distance of the Fasig-Tipton office at 3 East 48th Street, Manhattan. Never before in all my fifty years had I gone "out" to work. My base of operations had always been my home, on a farm or in a stable. To me, there was an amusing side: for the first time in my life I was going to work like a regular businessman—and I was vice-president of the company.

I never intended any move that I've made in my life. Most of them were happenstance. But I have never, never regretted making a move. You go to take the next step and there it is. I've certainly never had any second thoughts about assuming full-time duties with Fasig-Tipton.

My father, Rev. William Henry Finney, M.A., and mother, Laura Stanley Stone Finney. Lancashire, 1925.

My first trip back home on holiday. Edmund, Claud, and H.S.F. Alstonefield, Derbyshire, 1929.

The family: Olive, Marguerite, Patricia, John, and myself. Holly Beach Farm, Annapolis, Christmas 1934.

H. Guy Bedwell, America's leading trainer 1912–1917. Saratoga, 1919. *Photo by Cook, courtesy Keeneland Library.*

Tred Avon, the first foal I raised at Holly Beach Farm and a stakes winner of twenty-two races, with her first foal, a filly by Display. Holly Beach, 1933. *Photo courtesy Mrs. William T. Spence.*

Sylvester W. Labrot and Sylvester, Jr., on the lawn. Holly Beach, 1931. *Photo courtesy Mrs. William T. Spence.*

My first time in the ring for Fasig-Tipton: sale of C. V. Whitney Racing Stable in the paddock at Pimlico. Baltimore, November 1937.

"Fair exchange" of hats while judging at British War Relief Horse Show. Pikesville, Maryland, 1942. *Photo courtesy Mershon Master Made and Natural Action Photographs.*

Mounted Patrolmen of the U.S. Coast Guard in training. Wabasso, Florida, 1943.

First of the Hollywood extravaganzas. Selling under the lights at Santa Anita, Mayer Dispersal Sale. Los Angeles, February 1947. *Photo by Bert Clark Thayer.*

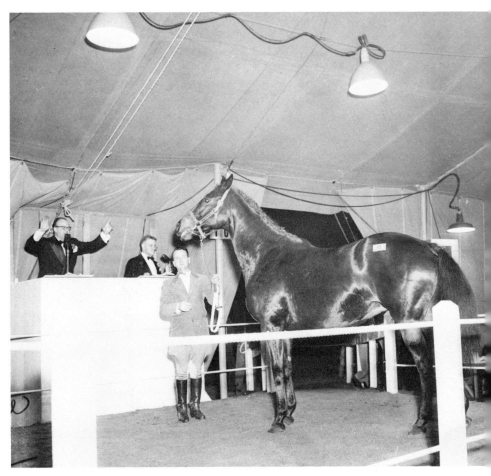

Second Mayer Sale, at Hollywood Park. In the ring, two-year-old Mailed Fist, who sold for $40,000. Los Angeles, January 1948.

Robert Sterling Clark and George Blackwell, a great yearling judge. Keeneland, 1950. *Photo courtesy Lexington, Ky.* Herald-Leader.

At the Hanover Bank, 1955. *Photo by Peter Stackpole, courtesy* Time-Life.

THE HANOVER BANK

Jockey Club Chairman William Woodward, Calumet Farm Owner Warren Wright, and George D. Widener. Belmont Park, 1950. The bloodstock of all three was appraised by H.S.F. in later years. *Photo courtesy Bert and Richard Morgan Studio.*

William Woodward, Jr., whose untimely death in 1955 cut short a promising career. *Photo courtesy* The Thoroughbred Record.

The great racehorse and sire Nashua. *Photo by J.C. Skeets Meadors, courtesy Keeneland Library.*

SIX

Fantastic, Colossal, Titanic: The Mayer Sales

When Louis B. Mayer, of movie fame, let it be known early in 1947 that he was going to sell his horses, nearly everybody in the business wanted to get in on the deal. But it turned out to be Fasig-Tipton that handled the dispersal, and in the process I got some of the most valuable training in selling and speaking I've ever had in my life.

Louis B. Mayer got into racing in the thirties. He had brought MGM to pre-eminence, and now he was interested in some relaxation. But in building up his stable and stud he proceeded as he did in everything he undertook: he got the best he could buy. He began by getting the best advice. His chief adviser on racing matters was Neil McCarthy, a brilliant lawyer and, in addition, a horseman—a polo player and Thoroughbred breeder. McCarthy knew where to go to get the best, and Mayer gave him a free hand.

Once it was even reported that in his pursuit of top racing class Mayer had offered Samuel D. Riddle a million dollars for Man o' War.

What actually happened, it seems, was that Mayer had said he'd give a million dollars to have a horse like Man o' War, and an ambitious young assistant of his thought he'd be very smart and took it upon himself to make the offer. Mr. Riddle was furious and made a public statement that Man o' War wasn't for sale at any price. Mr. Mayer, equally furious, denied flat out that he'd ever made such an offer. But the whole thing got tremendous coverage on radio and in the newspapers.

Eventually the pressures of the movie business came into conflict with the demands, and pleasures, of racing; and Mr. Mayer reluctantly decided to part with most of his horses.

At the time I was assistant to Kenneth Gilpin, president of Fasig-Tipton. I had met Mr. Mayer casually a few years before, when he bought Thumbs Up at Saratoga. The colt, bred in the purple (by Blenheim II out of Gas Bag, by Man o' War) had a slight knock on him because he had a little curb in his left hock; but Neil McCarthy advised Mayer to buy him in spite of the defect. He acquired a very useful piece of property: Thumbs Up won the Santa Anita Handicap and many other races.

I could hardly say that I knew Mr. Mayer, however, until we began discussing the sale of his stock. In my capacity as assistant to Major Gilpin, I made a quick trip to California to see Mr. Mayer and Neil McCarthy and also to inspect the stock—an inspection that left me greatly impressed. I had rarely seen such a good, sound lot of race-horses. Mayer had about forty two-year-olds in training, nine three-year-olds, and a group of older horses that included the big names of the stable: Busher, Be Faithful, Honeymoon, Grandmere, Battant, Burning Dream, and Stepfather. Mayer's broodmares and yearlings were equally impressive.

I strongly recommended a public sale, pointing out that Fasig-Tipton was the only sales company of consequence operating on a national—actually, international—basis. I also mentioned that if Mayer sold the stock to a syndicate, many of the friends that he'd like to see get some of his horses might be shut out. Mayer was polite, but non-committal. Later, however, he called me and said he wanted to go ahead with the auction. When the news got out, a headline in the

Morning Telegraph commented, "Humphrey Finney Puts Over Biggest Deal of Career."

Shortly afterwards I received a call from Alvord and Alvord, Mayer's tax advisers, asking me to come to Washington to discuss the sale. As we studied the matter in the light of Mr. Mayer's wishes, it became clear that a series of sales would be the best procedure. We agreed that the horses of racing age would be disposed of at the first sale, which we decided to stage on February 27, 1947, at Santa Anita.

A mix-up in hotel reservations just after I got to California for the sale led to an additional piece of business that made my trip to the Coast worthwhile to the Maryland Horse Breeders as well as to Fasig-Tipton. I had met John "Trader" Clark at the races at Santa Anita and found that he didn't have a hotel room so I invited him to share mine.

About five o'clock in the morning I woke up. Clark was on the telephone, talking to his brother in Kentucky. "I've just got an option on Occupy for $50,000," I heard him say.

I was wide awake. I got up on one elbow and said, "I'll take the option!" Clark stared at me for a moment, then finished his phone conversation. (Later, describing the incident, he said, "I thought the son-of-a-bitch was asleep.")

Occupy, by the great stallion Bull Dog out of Miss Bunting, by Bunting, was then six years old. A brilliant sprinter, he had won big races as a two-year-old. In the next two or three days I was busy on the telephone, trying to find one man, or a group of men, who would put up $50,000 to bring Occupy to Maryland. Trader Clark was dickering with two other people all the while.

Finally, when my option had less than a day to run, Harry Straus, president of the Maryland Horse Breeders Association, wired me that the Mercantile Trust of Baltimore had made the funds available to him. And that was how Maryland got Occupy. Harry Straus retained two shares in the horse, and a week after I got home from the Mayer sales I had sold eighteen more shares. Occupy was the first stallion syndicated in Maryland, and the second anywhere. (Beau Père, syndicated by Leslie Combs II, was the first.) By 1973 standards the Occupy transaction was peanuts, as nowadays anything under a million doesn't even make news, but it attracted considerable attention at the time.

Before I left the East Coast Major Gilpin had given me my instructions on this sale. "I don't care if Fasig-Tipton doesn't make a penny," he said, "but I want this to be the best-staged sale that's ever been run. Everything must be first class." But as it turned out, it was the easiest sale I ever had to arrange.

To handle publicity I went to Fred Purner, Santa Anita's public relations man. "I want you to handle the public relations for this event," I told him. "Put on a bang-up dinner, with an open bar up in the press box. Invite the visiting press and all your California men. And not just the ones that cover racing—get your society reporters, your movie reporters, columnists, everybody. It's in your hands. Do it right."

I didn't know anything about illumination, and there were no lights in the Santa Anita stands and parking lots. But MGM gave me their best lighting men, people experienced in lighting huge movie sets and outdoor scenes. They put floodlights everywhere and spotlights where they were needed, making the whole place as bright as daylight: the entrance to the track, the paths used in bringing the horses into the ring, the ring itself and the seating area. It cost a lot but it was effective.

The insurance to take over the property for that one night was $6,000. That was part of our contract with Santa Anita: we had to assume the cost of liability, fire and other insurance for the time we had the use of the property. We had elaborate catalogues printed, with pictures of the horses and much more information than is found in the standard sales catalogue. In all, the cost of putting on the sale was over $70,000; but the net profit to the company, after all expenses had been paid, was $40,000.

Purner did a masterful job with the publicity. We had the greatest press ever given a horse sale. And part of the sale was broadcast nationwide—the first time in history such a sale was put on radio. NBC had called, asking if they could schedule the selling of Busher, Honeymoon, Stepfather and Be Faithful to fit into a 15-minute period. I told them that we'd group these horses and do the best we could. NBC then set up a schedule that called for nationwide coverage for a quarter of an hour. On the entire West Coast, the sale was kept on the air for two hours.

I had never seen the general public take so much interest in a sale. To the people of Lexington, Kentucky, and Saratoga Springs, horse sales are an important part of their civic life, but this was different. Even for Hollywood the Mayer sale was something big, new, and glamorous. A Pasadena paper observed that 40,000 might have been on hand if attendance hadn't been by invitation only. And newspaper writers were caught up in the spell of it. Many of the reporters assigned to it were covering what was for them a new field, but what they wrote indicated that they were enjoying the experience. Press coverage was of unprecedented volume and character—what you might expect for an important sports event.

The sale certainly was an important Hollywood social event. Many celebrities of the film and entertainment world were present, up to and including Louella Parsons herself. Some were even successful bidders, like George Brent, Harry James and Jimmy Durante, who observed, "It's not far from Hollywood to Santa Anita as the dough flies."

The sale started at 7:30 p.m. "In my pocket" I had $250,000 of Eastern money, but I never got a chance to spend it. One would-be purchaser had instructed me to go as high as $50,000 for Honeymoon, but the bidding opened at $50,000, and Harry M. Warner got her for $135,000. I had $75,000 to put out for Be Faithful. At least I got into the bidding on that one, but E. E. Dale Shaffer went to $100,000 to get the fine mare. Mr. Warner paid the top price of the sale for Stepfather—$200,000. Neil S. McCarthy bought Busher for $135,000.

Here is how the auction team looked to the California audience, according to Ned Cronin of the Los Angeles *Times*:

> The famed auctioneering team of Humphrey S. Finney and George Swinebroad was imported to handle the bidding business. Finney, the No. 1 Thoroughbred auction expert in the world, is a disarming character, right out of Dickens. He comes complete with low-cut spectacles that sit right on the end of his beezer, and, with his Charles Laughton accent and manner, could talk a Salvation Army lassie out of her drum.
>
> His colleague, Swinebroad, is the direct opposite. A big booming guy with a corn-pone drawl, George alternately roars, cajoles,

jokes and fumes in his role as auctioneer. Between the two of them, they can empty the wallets of a crowd quicker than a crew of pickpockets.

As for Louis B. Mayer himself, Vincent X. Flaherty of the Los Angeles *Examiner* wrote about his reactions:

Louis B. Mayer sat high at the top of Santa Anita's blue-green Turf Club last night and listened while a man named George Swine-broad, a leather-lunged auctioneer with a rampant Kentucky accent, sold Mayer's magnificent stable.

He sat there—and he said little as his great horses were led into the auctioneer's ring . . .

Mayer sat there quietly, with his head down, listening intently to the singsong bedlam of the auctioneer's voice. He lifted his head once in a while to gaze down there upon the platinum glow of spotlights where his horses were going under the hammer . . .

Mayer had a drink of straight bourbon whiskey before him. Mayer doesn't drink. But he touched the glass and spun it around and pushed it away and spun it around again. His eyes were mirrored with mist . . . As far back against the wall as he could go Mayer sat . . . and, at the next table, sat beautiful Gail Patrick with a pair of field glasses.

And Mayer stared at her and stared at the untouched drink of bourbon on the table before him. He said he didn't feel very good about the big show, the circus of worked-up people and the wild auctioneer down on the track before him. He hated to see this happen. . . . [He was] wholly unable to join in with the spirit of the thing.

As for me, when it was all over I felt like an actor after a big first-night performance. We had sold sixty horses for a record $1,553,500, with an average of $25,891. And the notices were excellent, so I figured the show had been a smash hit.

I was in for a shock. The next day I saw Mayer's business manager, Myron Fox, and he didn't look like a man who had been a partner in the staging of a super-production. "Mr. Mayer isn't happy," Fox informed me.

I just about dropped dead. This had been what I thought was the sale of the century, and Mr. Mayer wasn't happy. Worse, Fasig-Tipton had the contract for only one sale. There were four more coming up: two-year-olds, foals of '46, were to be sold in '48; in December of that year, seventy or eighty broodmares were to go on the block; early in 1949, we were to sell the foals of '47; and in '50 the foals of '48 were to be offered. If Mr. Mayer wasn't happy, I wanted to know why, so I went to see him.

His office was very elaborately furnished. Every inch of the walls was covered with beautifully-framed photos of famous movie stars, autographed, "To dear Louis from So-and-so, in appreciation." But I didn't feel much like looking at pictures of pretty movie people.

Mr. Mayer confirmed that he wasn't happy. Even though the sale had brought half a million dollars more than he expected, he said, he wasn't at all pleased with the presentation. The horses were not properly shown—in the manner of a Mayer production. There had been too much rushing.

I explained that we sold the sixty horses as fast as we did only because the night was cold, people were starting to leave and we didn't want to lose any potential buyers. But it was evident that Mr. Mayer had gotten the idea that Swinebroad was out to set a record for selling the most horses in the shortest possible time. This wasn't true at all, of course; we were selling horses the way we knew how to sell them.

"Mr. Mayer," I said, "we can sell your horses any way you want them sold. If you want them sold one way, that's the way we'll sell them. If you want them another way, we'll sell them that way. I am a man of open mind; I'm not bound to any special routine, simply be cause that's *always* been the way a thing was done."

"All right," he said. "Thank you very much."

The interview was over. I had gotten nowhere. I went back East feeling very unhappy myself.

Just at that time, Mr. W. H. LaBoyteaux, Kenneth Gilpin's partner in the Fasig-Tipton Company, died, and shortly afterward, Major Gilpin, who had a history of heart disease, died too. His son, McGee Tyson Gilpin, was made president of the company. He had spent a lifetime with horses, and had been associated with his father in selling them.

We immediately began to think how we could sew up the rest of the Mayer sales. Mayer had been willing to talk to Major Gilpin, head of the company and a nationally-known horse breeder and consignor; the movie magnate, after all, was used to dealing with head men. It occurred to me that he would rather deal with a president than with an "assistant to the president," who *could* be nothing more than the guy who carries the briefcase. So we tried to set up an interview for Tyson with Mr. Mayer.

"No," came the reply. "I'm not going to talk to a kid."

Then I got the idea of asking Henry L. Knight to buy Mr. LaBoyteaux's interest in the company. Knight was a Kentuckian who had stuck with the Saratoga Sales when other Bluegrass breeders abandoned the Spa for Keeneland. He was a big breeder and "Knight's Night" was a tradition of the Saratoga Sales. Knight was someone I thought Mr. Mayer might be willing to deal with.

Tyson liked the idea, and Knight immediately saw the advantages of buying into Fasig-Tipton. Moreover, he was very willing to go after Mayer—who, as it turned out, received him as a person on the same economic plateau and a peer in the world of business. The result was that I got a call from Henry. "You'd better come on out to California," he said. "Mr. Mayer wants to see you." So off I went to the West Coast for another session with the "Hollywood Rajah."

"I've been checking up on you," Mayer began. "I feel that I know more about you." He had a lot of respect for British people, he said. He explained that he had some good ones with him in the movie business, and he liked them very much. "There is only one type of person in the world I can't do business with," he continued, "and that is the man who tells me he can't do a thing, or won't try a new way to accomplish something just because it's never been done that way before. Now, you said," he reminded me, "that you're a man with an open mind."

"Yes, I did," I agreed.

"Well," he said, "so am I. I came here to Hollywood and I revolutionized the motion picture business. People said, 'Mayer's doing this,' and 'Mayer's doing that. He'll go broke. He'll kill the business.' All those people are working for me now.

"I took Spencer Tracy out of a fishing boat in Catalina, and we had to teach him to talk. He became a great actor. Clark Gable was a lineman for the telephone company when we took him. We had to teach *him* to talk. Now he's 'The King.'

"Now you're a foreigner. Have you ever realized that we have to make foreigners speak more slowly in pictures than we do native Americans?"

I had not.

"The reason," he went on, "is that if you're watching a picture the impulse is from your eyes to your brain. If your ears get the message at the same time, you get the whole story—you enjoy the picture. But if somebody is talking with a Scotch burr and you have difficulty understanding it, your eyes are running ahead of your ears. What you hear isn't keeping up with what you see, so you *don't* get the whole story, and you can't possibly enjoy the picture. To compensate for this hearing lag, any actor with a foreign or different accent must speak more slowly. You're an Englishman and you have good diction; but you've got to speak more slowly."

That was one of the things Mr. Mayer taught me. But the lesson wasn't over. "You say you have to sell horses quickly to get them sold," he went on. "You're only partly right. When you're selling horses that are going to bring $10,000 or less, you shouldn't waste time over them. But when you've got a sister to Honeymoon, or a brother to Stepfather, *then* you go after the people individually. You see that Mr. Warner is interested in this one, and he should be because he's got the brother, a topflight racehorse. And you see that someone else is interested, so you play one against another. 'Mr. X,' you say, 'you're not going to let Mr. Y take this horse away at that price,' and you tell Mr. X what the horse can do for him."

Now sales announcers and auctioneers have been playing one bidder against another since the birth of the business, but Mr. Mayer's idea was to create rivalries between buyers where none had existed before. He did not overlook the tiniest point, and he utilized psychological factors that showed his genius. For instance, he seated the big bidders—or the ones he expected would be big bidders—where they could see one another. With that arrangement, a man wasn't merely bidding on a horse, he was engaging in a fight and watching his opponent's moves. Every bid was a punch, and the next one could be the knockout punch.

But Mayer still had something on his mind, and what he said now really jolted me. "Your auctioneer," he declared, "is hopeless. A lot of people can't understand that Kentucky voice of his. Now, he's supposed to be the star of the show, but you're the director. You have to make him do what you want him to do."

The auctioneer was the respected George Swinebroad, considered just about the best in the business by just about everybody *in* the business.

When George arrived in California, he asked, "Have you seen Mr. Mayer?"

"Yeah," I said.

"Does he want to see me?" he asked.

"No."

"Well, what did he say?" George persisted.

"He said," I told him, "you stink."

That wasn't a very nice way to put it, but I wasn't feeling very nice at the time. A man of great pride in his work, George was stunned. But then I told him the substance of my conversation with Mr. Mayer. Swinebroad pondered for a while, then said, "Me and you can sell 'em any way he wants 'em sold."

The next auction on the agenda was the sale of two-year-olds of 1948. We went over the horses and agreed on the ones that were likely to be the headliners. My practice has always been to appraise the horses before a sale, establishing what I consider the "right" price for each. Sometimes I'm too optimistic and sometimes I underrate a horse's sales potential, but at least I have a basis to work from.

It was apparent that we could easily take our time with this sale. There were only thirty-nine horses, as against sixty in the first sale, and we had the same amount of time. And many of the thirty-nine were brothers and sisters of the ones we'd sold the year before, which, with two or three exceptions, hadn't done much since. Further, we'd had Honeymoon, Busher and Stepfather in the first sale—a real star cast —but there was a conspicuous lack of star quality the second time around.

While we were contemplating the possibility of a less spectacular box office, the Old Man (as we had begun to call Mr. Mayer behind his back) sent for me.

"What do you think of Free France?" he asked.

"Well," I told him, "he's a wind-broken horse—won a minor stakes or two—but he's the best-looking son of Man o' War. And, of course, he's out of La France, by Sir Gallahad III. There isn't any better breeding."

Mayer had bought Free France to get a son of Man o' War, and ten of his progeny, all members of his first crop, were in this sale.

"He's the best-looking son of Man o' War," Mayer repeated after me, and I could see he was thinking.

"In appearance," I added, "he's the most like Man o' War of all his sons."

"Well, you know, most of these people never saw Man o' War," Mayer pointed out. "What do you think of bringing Free France up from the farm and parading him in the ring?" He shoved his hands into his pockets and leaned back, seeing a mental picture. "You're in the ring," he said, "and you're the announcer, and you're saying, 'Now gentlemen and ladies, some of you never saw Man o' War. Now here is the truest son of the horse many call America's greatest. . . . '"

I picked up the pitch: "And he is out of La France, a daughter of the super-sire Sir Gallahad III, and La France is also the dam of Johnstown who won the Kentucky Derby and the Belmont Stakes in a year that was jam-packed with good three-year-olds. And La France also produced Jacola, a great racemare who beat Seabiscuit in the Laurel Stakes in '38, and Jacola was the dam of Phalanx."

Mayer was enthusiastic. "You go ahead and tell them that," he said.

I left, feeling confident that *this* time we would run the sale in a manner that would satisfy Mr. Mayer.

Our morale had been given a big boost after the first sale when Swinebroad and I received a letter from Frank Capra's casting department asking us to appear in the film "Broadway Bill," starring Bing Crosby. The script called for an auction, and George and I were to sell a horse to Bing. Capra's proposal made me feel that even though Mr. Mayer had been disappointed in our presentation, the first sale couldn't have been a complete flop from a dramatic point of view.

Sale No. 2 had a different setting: a big tent at Hollywood Park. Since there was no racing at Hollywood at the time, we had stabling facilities hard by the ring. Capra wanted to witness the sale, so Tyson Gilpin gave him a tour of the place and described the whole operation early in the day. Long before the action started, Capra knew just about what to expect, and during the sale was able to observe audience reaction and whatever else directors look for.

Again the press coverage was "colossal," as they used to say in the screen capital.

"Fantastic Hollywood Spends More Than Million on 39 Two-Year-Olds," was the headline in the Los Angeles *Herald-Express* of January 13, 1948.

We started the show by parading Free France. He might not have been the greatest stallion in the world by a long shot, but you couldn't tell it by looking at him. Man o' War himself could not have caused much more of a stir. Free France was a star, at least for a day, and he got a reception worthy of a star—a rousing round of applause. His appearance, plus the fact that the crowd was geared up for something big, contributed, I am sure, to the success of the sale. Free France's ten two-year-olds alone brought $161,500.

This was all the more remarkable because Free France's racing record, as I've said, was nothing to make Leslie Combs run out and throw a syndicate together. The day after the sale old Woody Fitzgerald, who trained Gallant Sir and other horses for Norman Church, stopped me at Santa Anita. "Who had the idea of bringing that gawdam thing up and dragging him around the ring?" he wanted to know. "Well, it had to be Mayer," he went on. "I needn't have asked. But it don't make no difference. Those so-and-sos ought to average about $3,500, and instead they average $16,000! There oughta be a law."

A high point of excitement during the sale was reached when a bidding duel occurred between Harry M. Warner and Lou Bronstein for Doctrine, Stepfather's brother. Warner had paid $200,000 for Stepfather at the first Mayer sale, and the feeling was that he would go all out for Doctrine. But he stopped at $65,000.

All in all, the thirty-nine two-year-olds brought $1,033,250, with an average of $26,493.50—a record. Imperial Rock, an Alibhai colt who was a full brother to the good racehorse Solidarity, brought $70,000, the most ever paid for a two-year-old sold at public auction. Pedigree, a full brother to Honeymoon, went for $68,000, and Doctrine brought $67,000.

But despite all the high prices, I was worrying all evening whether or not *this* one would please Mayer. It was worry wasted. After the sale, Mayer came across the ring beaming, with tears in his eyes and his hand up in sort of a Hitlerian salute. He grabbed me with one hand and George with the other.

"Boys," he announced joyously, "you were diamonds to nickels to what you were last year!"

We had sold horses for very good prices, but that wasn't what made Louis B. happy. What stirred his soul was the fact that the presentation had been made the way he wanted it—with the proper showmanship. He was a stickler for having everything just right, and that was the way he wanted the sale—worthy of being called a Louis B. Mayer production.

He showed his satisfaction in a more practical way than just, "Well played, Harrow!" He awarded Fasig-Tipton the contracts to sell the remainder of his stock. And he sent me a note in which he declared that "You are not only a gentleman, but you are turning out to be a first class scholar as well."

In the third sale, held in January 1949, we disposed of the brood-mares. By that time, Mayer sales had become a feature of Hollywood life. Celebrities came out, some to enjoy the show or to show themselves, but others to participate in the bidding. Again, the newspaper coverage was extensive.

Out of that sale, I bought Winkle II for Mrs. Marion duPont Scott. The mare was carrying Jampol, who turned out to be a very good runner. Winkle was a good producer. At a subsequent sale, I bought another of her daughters, Your Game, for Mrs. George L. Harrison. Your Game, like her dam, became a first-class producer.

And it was at that sale that William Goetz, Mayer's son-in-law, bought Your Host for $20,000. This seems like a trifle, but at the time Your Host didn't look much like a horse that was going to win $384,795 and to sire Kelso, one of the great horses of all time.

My work with Mr. Mayer unquestionably was of extreme value to me in the years that followed. The experience was helpful to me in selling, but even more so in determining the kind of presentation that should be made at a given sale, and it certainly helped me improve my public speaking. I had thought I knew something about using public address systems, and I got along well enough making speeches, but I learned a whole lot more by being around Mr. Mayer and getting the benefit of his coaching.

Incidentally, if you didn't see Swinebroad and me in Bing's picture, there was a reason for that: we weren't in it. The sale scene was cut out of the script, depriving the cinema-loving public of the chance to view the histrionics of another Gable and Tracy.

When we held the final sale for Mr. Mayer in 1950, he was a very sick man, making regular trips to San Francisco for medical treatment. Actually, he was dying. He succumbed to leukemia a short time later.

SEVEN

Never Say Die
and His Master

My association with Robert Sterling Clark began shortly after Admiral Cary T. Grayson died in 1938. The admiral had guided Mr. Clark in his U.S. Thoroughbred ventures and had kept the horses on his Blue Ridge Farm, in Upperville, Virginia. Earlier, Mr. Clark had bought a farm in Kentucky and spent a fortune on horses, but things didn't go very well for him. He became disgusted, shook the dust of the Blue Grass State from his feet and sent his horses to Blue Ridge. After Admiral Grayson died, Mr. Clark talked with Mrs. Grayson, and asked her to suggest someone to look after his racing interests in America. Mrs. Grayson recommended me.

Mr. Clark had bought part of Admiral Grayson's Virginia farm, but he didn't have many horses at the time—a few runners in New England with Matt Smart, and some mares at Blue Ridge. The only one of these of special interest was Ancona, which later became the dam of Colchis.

At the request of Mr. Clark, I went down to Upperville for a talk.

He was a wonderful host and a great epicure, and, after a magnificent dinner, he asked me if I would look after all his stock in America and relieve him of the responsibilities. I told him I would.

So that was the start of it. I was on Mr. Clark's payroll until the early '50s, when he cut down his American activities, put his brood-mares at John A. Bell III's Jonabell Farm at Lexington, Kentucky, and did his racing abroad. I continued on a consultation fee basis until shortly before Mr. Clark's death.

When I started with Mr. Clark, we made a purchase here or there to help build up his broodmare band. Then, in 1938, Mr. Clark got very keen on researching the old American bloodlines. He wanted to revive the old line of Lexington, which was pretty dead, and the line of Glencoe. There had been some Lexington blood in California and Nevada, planted there by Theodore Winters and Lucky Baldwin. From Baldwin's Santa Anita Stud came the great speed of Lady Josephine that resulted in Mahmoud (she was his third dam) and heaven knows how many prominent speed horses in Europe and America today.

I went West, and Olive and I drove all over California and Nevada, looking for some of this old blood. I finally found two fillies just north of Carson City, Nevada, on the old Winters Ranch. One was by a horse named Joe Hooker, out of a mare by Joe Hooker, and the other was by Joe Hooker, out of a mare by the sire of Joe Hooker. They were trim, clean-looking and sound, and had some white splashes like Rex Ellsworth's famous Candy Spots. But, in no other way did they resemble Candy Spots. I'm glad they didn't cost much.

I picked up another mare, California Ada, by Cruzados, that traced back to Emperor of Norfolk—real Baldwin breeding. Mr. Clark sent California Ada to England, and was quite upset when the owner of one of the top sires refused her a mating.

He was a great man for experimenting, and I never tried to talk him out of an idea. It was his money. The only thing I could do was tell him what I thought the odds against success would be. Then I'd go ahead and do everything I could to try to prove him right. That way, if the experiment turned out to be a flop, he was quite ready to accept it as a flop. A failure didn't matter, provided he was convinced that everything possible had been done to test his theory.

After the fall of France and before America entered World War

II, Mr. Clark decided to look for a place in the West. He was sure this country was going to get into the war, and there was the possibility that the East Coast would be bombed. In such an eventuality, he figured he'd ship his horses west and hold them there for the duration of the war. I went out to Colorado with him; we searched the state over and found a nice farm near Colorado Springs. He gave up the idea shortly afterward, when he reappraised the situation and concluded that America wasn't going to be invaded from the east.

With the Germans advancing, the next problem was to get the Clark horses out of France and England and into America. Of course, all ships going to Europe were loaded with material we were sending to the Allies, but there was room on ships returning to the United States. The British Bloodstock Agency shipped three or four horses a week on vessels of the American Merchant Line. We got some very important shipments. In one load, we got Galaday, dam of Galatea II, winner of the Oaks and 1,000 Guineas. Galaday had been purchased as a foal from A. B. Hancock, for $5,000. She was by Sir Gallahad III and she was a foundation mare. From her descended many top-class racehorses in both America and England.

Mr. Clark had hoped to run Galatea in the St. Leger—she was that kind of a filly—even though she would have had to meet the mighty Blue Peter, Lord Rosebery's Derby winner. I don't think Blue Peter ever was really pushed to the limit on the racecourse. My feeling is that he would have been favored over Galatea, though this is mere supposition, as no St. Leger was run in 1939.

In that shipment with Galaday was her two-year-old daughter, a filly named Boreale, by Vatout, a St. Simon line horse. We got back eighteen or twenty horses, in all—the best of the Clark racehorses and the mares that were in England. Among the racehorses that were brought to America were Abbe Pierre, Saguenay II and Trois Pistoles.

Mr. Clark told me to hire a trainer. He wanted to have his own trainer and his own setup. So I went to "Sunny Jim" Fitzsimmons, who trained for Belair Stud and the Phipps family, and asked him if he could let me have a man. Mr. Fitz was a wonderful person—he trained many good men, like Al Robertson, who went with Eddie Neloy, after Eddie took over the Phipps horses. Vince Mara had been with Sunny Jim for a long time and was one of his foremen. What Mr. Clark was offering was a good opportunity for a capable trainer, and Vince was that, so Mr. Fitz said, "Take him."

Vince did very well with the Clark horses. We sent them to Laurel to get some education in American racing. Foreign horses have to become accustomed to racing on dirt, and having it thrown back in their faces. If they are not given this experience, they'll duck out or quit running the first time they feel that barrage—and that goes double if the track is off when the stuff comes in clods.

The best horse Vince Mara trained for us was a bay colt out of Ancona, a blind mare. Ancona had been on Blue Ridge Farm during a year when there were many cases of periodic ophthalmia. Quite a number of Mr. Clark's mares went blind. It's a curious thing, twenty or thirty years ago, you'd see a tremendous number of mares that had gone blind with ophthalmia. Now, you rarely come across one on a stud farm.

Because of convenience, Ancona was bred to Happy Argo, which stood at Blue Ridge. Ancona was by Toro, out of Flying Field, a Campfire mare Mr. Clark had bred. The foal that resulted from her breeding to Happy Argo was Colchis. We had another colt of moderate expectations, you might say, so we gelded both of them. Mr. Clark believed in gelding colts he didn't think were going to be of top class for stud, a practice followed with success by the great trainer, Andrew Jackson Joyner.

Colchis was a rough bay, with a big curb on his right hock, and a small, sharp curb on his left hock. One day, Mr. Clark said, "Finney, I don't think there is much use keeping those two geldings. See if you can 'out' the pair." He had a great expression. We'd go through the place and he'd say, "Let's out this one. Out it." And that was it. If he said, "Out it," the horse had to go.

Nobody would give me $500 apiece for them, even on the cuff, with money to be paid out of winnings. So we kept the pair, and Vince took them over and trained them. Colchis turned out to be a real decent horse. He dead-heated with Alsab in the Eastern Shore at Havre de Grace in 1941, as a two-year-old, and he beat Alsab in the Chesapeake Trial and the Chesapeake Stakes the next spring. Five times he went up against Alsab, winning two, losing two and dead-heating once.

As Alsab was one of the top horses of his time, we thought Colchis had done pretty well. He was fourth in the Preakness, which Alsab won, with Sun Again and Requested dead-heating for second place. George Woolf rode Colchis in the Preakness and Mr. Clark was so tickled with the fourth-place finish that he gave Woolf $2,000, the entire amount that Colchis earned for fourth money. Colchis won a few more races, and then was retired to a life of ease on the farm where he lived fifteen or eighteen years.

Boreale won a race at Belmont and bowed, so to stud she went. We discussed suitable mates and I recommended War Admiral. "He's got everything she hasn't got," I said, "out-cross, pedigree and he isn't too big." He was in great shape at the time.

Singing Grass, a chestnut filly, came out of that pairing. She was a useful runner, winning several handicaps in England. When she was retired, Gerald McElligott of the British Bloodstock Agency, who managed Clark's horse interests in England, insisted that Nasrullah was the stallion for her. Singing Grass was returned to America in foal to Nasrullah, and Never Say Die was foaled in 1951, on Jonabell Farm, in Kentucky.

The colt was sent to England and was trained by Joe Lawson, at Newmarket.

When Never Say Die won the 1954 Epsom Derby, Mr. Clark was in the hospital. He had lived in New York most of his life, so when the news of the Derby victory came over the wires, turf writers and sports editors tried to find him. Nobody knew where he was. His name wasn't listed in the phone book. He didn't have an office in New York—just a desk in his attorney's office on Wall Street. John Chandler, who was the Associated Press's racing editor at that time, called me to see if I could put him in communication with Mr. Clark. Right afterwards, Miss Catherine Dwyer, Mr. Clark's secretary, called up and said the newspapers were after her trying to get information about Mr. Clark. One of the papers had called Clark's farm in Virginia, and somebody there gave them the number of the Wall Street office. That's how they found Miss Dwyer. (Never underrate the persistence and resourcefulness of the men of the press.)

Anyway, I said, "Where is the boss?"

"He's in the hospital," she replied.

"What's wrong with him?"

"Oh, he's just having a checkup," she said, and then asked, "What am I to tell people?"

"Well," I said, "we'd better get a statement from Mr. Clark."

I called the hospital, and got hold of the old man. When I told him Never Say Die had won the Epsom Derby, he sort of grunted.

"Mr. Clark," I said, "you've got to give a statement to the press. They're worrying the life out of Miss Catherine."

"Oh don't bother," was Mr. Clark's response. "Don't tell them anything."

"Mr. Clark," I argued, "you don't realize what you've done. You've done what many American breeders have tried to do and failed. William Woodward has never been able to win an Epsom Derby. You have."

That might have hit home, because he had no use for Woodward. Clark had had a great battle with The Jockey Club when Woodward was chairman. So, he said, "All right, tell them anything you want to tell them. Give all credit to McElligott; he planned the breeding."

I called the turf dailies, Chandler of the AP and other services and papers that were interested.

The next problem that arose was the need of a photograph. Nobody had a picture of this man who had won many races in the U.S. and in France and England, and who was a successful breeder and a prominent art collector. I called Miss Dwyer again, and she said she didn't know of any picture anywhere of Mr. Clark. Then she remembered that a photo somebody had taken in a restaurant was at the Clark apartment. Again, I called Mr. Clark.

"The newspapers want your picture," I told him.

"Oh, no—no photographs," he barked.

"Mr. Clark," I explained, "you don't seem to comprehend. You can't get behind a bush now. You're the only American who's ever bred and owned the winner of the Epsom Derby. American-breds have won it, and American-owned or leased horses have won it; but, in the 174 years of the race's history, you're the only American who has bred and owned a Derby winner."

While he was mulling that over, I said, "How about that picture that's up on the mantelpiece in your apartment?"

"Oh," he said, "my wife doesn't like it."

I kept pushing.

Finally, he gave in. "All right," he told me, "you can have it."

I sent Bruce Collins from my Fasig-Tipton office on 48th Street for the picture. Miss Dwyer called ahead and told the French maid to let Bruce have the picture, and Bruce kept the cab waiting for his return trip. I called the AP, the *Herald-Trib* and the *Times*. They sent cameramen over and they photographed the photograph of Mr. Clark on my desk. And that's the only picture there was.

The immensity of his accomplishment and its importance in racing must have dawned on Mr. Clark after a while, for, during the afternoon, Miss Dwyer called me. "Mr. Clark wants you to come over," she announced. "We're going to have a celebration. Come up at four o'clock."

So I went to Doctor's Hospital for the party. Mr. Clark, up in the high seventies in years, was lying in his hospital bed. Mrs. Clark, a beautiful, white-haired lady, was with him. His lawyer, Mr. Roberts, also was on hand, and of course, Miss Dwyer.

Mrs. Clark had brought the champagne, and somebody produced soft paper cups. We toasted Never Say Die first. Then we drank to Lawson, the trainer, and McElligott and to John A. Bell III, at whose farm Never Say Die stood up and nursed, and to the seventeen-year-old jockey, Lester Piggott, who had ridden his first Derby winner.

How Never Say Die got his name is rather interesting. As everyone who has attempted to register a horse with The Jockey Club knows, all the good names seem to be taken. The owner sends in the ones he prefers (in order of preference) and The Jockey Club turns them down, because they're the names of horses that have appeared in the records within the last fifteen years. That's the rule—and, of course, names of "prominent" horses, no matter how long ago they raced, are not acceptable.

Mr. Clark had sent in fifteen or twenty names for the son of Nasrullah—Singing Grass. All had been turned down, and Mr. Clark was beginning to feel he'd never get a name for the colt. Miss Dwyer wasn't discouraged. "Oh, don't worry, Mr. Clark," she advised. "Never say die."

"That's it!" declared her employer. "That's it! We'll call him Never Say Die."

They rang up The Jockey Club and found that the name was

available, and immediately sent a messenger around to 250 Park Avenue with a letter requesting the name. A name can't be claimed over the telephone. So that's how the winner of the '54 Epsom Derby got his name.

In the fall of 1954, when I was recovering from a heart attack, Mr. Clark paid me a visit at my home in Rye, New York. Though he was tottery, he came upstairs and presented me with a fine color photo of Never Say Die, with Lester Piggott up. During his visit, Mr. Clark talked about Never Say Die. The colt looked a sure shot to win the Champion Stakes and that would have put Clark at the top of the owners' list in England. The Queen was close behind.

"Know what I did?" he asked.

Of course I didn't.

"After I saw Never Say Die win the St. Leger at Doncaster, I went over to France and sent McElligott a cable saying, 'Out everything. Take him out of everything.' In no time McElligott was on the phone raising hell and Lawson, my trainer, was very upset. Lawson never had won a Champion Stakes."

"Well, why *did* you take him out?" I asked.

"He's done everything," Mr. Clark said. "What was there for him to do?"

"You could have had the honor of being the leading owner and the leading breeder," I replied.

Then he said, "She should have it."

"You mean you didn't want to beat the Queen?" I asked.

"Well," he said, "I just had one horse that was doing everything, and I was lucky. He'd done all that was asked of him, and I didn't want to hurt him." It was a fine gesture.

Another fine gesture was Clark's presentation of Never Say Die to England. Actually, he gave the horse to the National Stud, which is operated by the government. The stipulation was made that ten breeding nominations be reserved annually for Irish breeders. The Minister of Agriculture accepted the horse in behalf of the government. In order to give away the horse, Mr. Clark had to pay a "gift" tax to the United States Government. I don't know exactly how much it was, but it was substantial. The horse was valued at $750,000.

"I just hope I can live to see his get run," he said, as much to himself as to me.

Mr. Clark did not live to see the progeny of Never Say Die perform on the track. He died when the members of the first crop were weanlings.

R. Sterling Clark left more than just the memory of Never Say Die's accomplishments. As an art collector, he acquired treasures of inestimable value. These were left to Williams College at Williamstown, Massachusetts. On the campus he built the Sterling and Francine Clark Art Institute, out of blocks of Vermont marble of tremendous thickness, and with two air-conditioning systems. In the building, among other things are thirty-two Renoirs, works of Degas, Picasso, Homer, Sargent, Stuart and Cassatt, bronzes by Rodin, Degas and Remington and many prints and silver *objets d'art.* There is also a fine library. It was all collected by Mr. Clark.

Mr. Clark also had a wonderful collection of racing books. There was a set of *Stud Books; Racing Manuals* beginning with the early '20s; and an entire set of the *English Racing Calendar,* going back into the eighteenth century. There was a set of *American Race Horses,* The Jockey Club series of five books covering the history of American racing, and a set of the *Bloodstock Breeders' Review* published by the British Bloodstock Agency (which started in 1912 and is the only worldwide history of horse racing kept current). Mr. Clark's collection of *Chart Books* went back to the time old man Brunell first started them, about 1900, and he had *Goodwin's Guides* covering an even earlier era.

All these sets of books were given to the Thoroughbred Club of America, in Lexington, Kentucky. The books are priceless and are used by students and outsiders as well as by club members. All of the books have been kept up to date.

Also given to the Thoroughbred Club were the books Mr. Clark had made up himself covering his own stock. Representing a tremendous amount of work were his own private stud book, pedigrees of his mares, and the horses he had raced and bought. These were entered in books by his own hand—traced back to the very beginning—ten or twelve generations. More than that, there were his comments about the animals. Some of these were very amusing. Mr. Clark's present of books formed the nucleus of the fine library the Thoroughbred Club has now. Other people have added to it, but it is still called the R. Sterling Clark Library.

Mr. Clark led a full and busy life, and was a very interesting person to be with. He was always trying to do things better, and loved to try any experiment he thought could be worthwhile. On the turf, he enjoyed successes that would have given unadulterated satisfaction to most men. But, even Never Say Die didn't completely satisfy him.

"If he'd only been the result of one of my experiments," he grieved. "After all, he was bred in the orthodox manner."

All I could say was, "It's a gawdam pity!"

EIGHT

The Woodward Sales

William Woodward, Sr. was a tall, dignified man, a respected Wall Street banker, and one of the great men of racing. His Belair Stud in Maryland, which went back to the 1700s, raced the great stars Gallant Fox, Omaha, Johnstown, Vagrancy, and many others. I used to see him at least once a year, usually in the spring during the Pimlico meetings. He was a host par excellence and a gracious and able man.

I remember taking Joe Palmer down to Belair to see him. Joe Palmer was the most brilliant racing writer of my generation—or perhaps any generation. I called Mr. Woodward and told him I'd like to bring Joe down to lunch and he said "You'll tell him the rules," and I said "Oh yes, don't worry about that." When we went in for lunch Mr. Woodward said, "Now Palmer, I suppose Finney's told you the rules. When you pass this portal, you're off the record." And Joe said, "Yessir, I understand that." Joe didn't think much of the austere aristocracy of The Jockey Club, of which Woodward was naturally a member and for some years Chairman, and he would sometimes poke fun at them in his nice way. But he really enjoyed that lunch.

When Woodward died in September 1953, I was called in to appraise his extensive Thoroughbred holdings for tax purposes. After this work was completed, John Ludewig, Woodward's secretary and co-executor of the estate with the Hanover Bank, called me to New York to discuss the appraisals with William Woodward, Jr. Bill, Jr. was thirty-four at the time, handsome, tall, outgoing—altogether a charming young man. He was an ex-naval officer, and a graduate of Groton and Harvard, his father's alma mater. A great tennis player, he was never seen around the racetrack. I heard that his first visit to the course was at Pimlico on the day Belair's Sabette won the Gallorette in 1953. So it was natural to think of him as a neophyte.

But it was wrong to do so. As it turned out, he knew all about his father's horses. I was tremendously impressed with his knowledge of what was going on. I had forgotten the exact date I had appraised the horses in Kentucky, but Bill knew.

I gave him my figures on the mares and foals, the yearlings and racing stock. The yearlings were at Belair Stud in Maryland, and a bay colt by Nasrullah, out of Segula, by Johnstown, was in the lot. I wish I could say that I put the highest price on that one, because he was destined to win $1,288,565, running under the name of Nashua. But I didn't. Nashua was second highest on the yearling appraisal, with my top figure going on a colt by the same sire, out of Hypnotic.

The big farm in Maryland was left to Bill, Jr., according to the terms of his father's will. Watching Sabette win, or becoming master of Belair or both, must have shown Bill that racing was a sport worthy of more attention. He became an interested participant in the game and, when Nashua began to show signs of greatness, the young man's enthusiasm mounted.

After Swaps beat Nashua in the Kentucky Derby, there was a great hue and cry for a match race between the two fine colts. Bill didn't push the project, but he was willing to go along, and enjoyed one of the thrills of his life when Eddie Arcaro on Nashua, beat Willie Shoemaker, on Swaps, at Washington Park. That was in '55, when Nashua earned $752,550, the most ever rolled up by a Thoroughbred in his three-year-old season. Damascus, owned by Mrs. Edith Bancroft, Bill's sister, bettered this in 1967 by bringing in $817,941—but the record was still in the family.

A bizarre tragedy ended young Bill's life in the autumn of 1955. He was killed by a shotgun blast in his own home when mistaken for an intruder. So, before William Woodward, Sr.'s estate was completely settled, I was appraising the estate of William Woodward, Jr., for the purpose of holding a dispersal sale of the stock.

I had to go to Lexington, early in November for the sale of Henry Knight's horses, and went over to Claiborne on November 5, to appraise the Woodward broodmares. I was in Maryland, at Belair Stud, on the seventh to put a price on the weanlings, and at Danny Shea's Merryland Farm, on the eighth, to evaluate the yearlings. On November 10—that was Thursday—I went to Aqueduct to look over the racing stock in order to be able to estimate its worth in dollars.

I returned to New York, to confer with Charles F. Mapes, of the Hanover Bank, and John Ludewig, on Monday, November 14. I had my figures and some recommendations ready. The executors wanted to sell everything as quickly as possible. They wanted to get the ultimate, with the least expense, but had no idea of the value of the horses. A. B. Hancock, Jr., of Claiborne Farm, where the mares were, had done an appraisal of the estate, in addition to the one I made. We found our figures were fairly close.

The horses were divided into three groups. Group A was Nashua, B was made up of nine racehorses and twelve yearlings, and C, a package of twenty-four broodmares and sixteen weanlings. Group D was all three rolled into one. I put a figure of $1,200,000 on Nashua, and thought the nine racehorses and twelve yearlings ought to bring $225,000. The twenty-four mares and sixteen weanlings I appraised at $475,000, for a total of $1,900,000. The trustees felt that if everything could be sold, promptly, at about the figures named, they would be doing very well.

The big problem, of course, was Nashua. He was the most valuable piece of Thoroughbred property that was available for sale in the world. No animal of that value had ever been offered at public auction. He had to be sold as quickly as possible, because of the ever-present danger of injury. He was being turned out daily in a paddock at Claiborne Farm, and horses are remarkably keen at thinking up ways to damage themselves. Furthermore, in an open sale of valuable stock, there is always the danger of collusion. Interested groups can get together and set the price before the sale—agree not to go above a certain figure, which might be a low one. I recommended that sealed bids be asked for on Nashua. The trust officers approved this idea and expanded it. They decided to sell all the horses that way, though I wanted them to go at auction.

December 15 was set as the date of the sale; bids had to be in by 11:00 a.m. on that date. The requirements were that a certified check for ten per cent of the amount offered was to accompany the bid, the balance to be paid within thirty days. Also, the executors reserved "the right to refuse any and all bids." This left an "out," in case the bids didn't come up to what we figured the horses were worth. Should that occur, they still could be offered in the sales ring. It was also made clear that "no examination with respect to Nashua's fertility has ever been made and none will be for the purpose of this sale; the Executors make no representation as to Nashua's potential ability as a stallion, the horse being offered as he stands."

Requiring a certified check for ten per cent of the amount bid kept out the jokers. We knew damned well that there would be a lot of screwballs who would send in all kinds of bids, if they didn't have to put up any money.

Some people wondered why Nashua wasn't tested for fertility, and thought that failure to take such a test might cause some potential buyers to shy away. But Nashua was then a three-year-old with, probably, another season's racing ahead of him, no matter who bought him. He had earned $945,415, and was absolutely sound. He had every chance in the world of hitting the million mark and of passing Citation to become the leading money-winner of the world (which, incidentally, he did). So we were not about to allow him to get upset by trying him on a test mare. The risk was too great, and the results of the test could be inconclusive. Nashua and all the other horses had been gone over carefully by competent veterinarians, and anyone interested could send his own vet. Further, we had a last-minute check of all the stock. At 11:00 a.m. on December 15, before the bids were opened, the results of the check were phoned in to us at the bank from the three locations where the horses were being kept. The final word was that the physical condition of all the animals was the same as when the sale had been announced. That, in itself, was a record of some kind. When you've had sixty-two horses on your hands for two months and not one of them manages to hurt himself, some kind of a miracle has taken place.

Advertisements describing the stock and explaining the conditions of the sale were placed in a number of newspapers. The popularity of Nashua, the unusual nature of the sale and the great value of the stock were all newsworthy, and press coverage spread far beyond the trade journals and the racing dailies.

There was great speculation as to what Nashua would bring. The estimates made by Bull Hancock and myself, of course, were not made public. They were made merely to give the executors some idea of the value of the property with which they were dealing. When I realized how much interest there was in Nashua, I began to think that my appraisal had been too low. I wouldn't have been surprised if he had brought two million.

Brigadier R. S. Scott, head of the British Bloodstock Agency, Fasig-Tipton's partner in England, called me one day in the interest of his client, Stavros Niarchos. Immensely wealthy, Niarchos was going into racing. My advice to him was to buy the whole lot. Then, he could keep what he wanted and sell the lesser lights. I told Scott that my appraisal had been a bit short of two million, and that if Niarchos was prepared to offer two million and perhaps a couple hundred thousand lagniappe, he was sure of getting the horses. I added that if he did this, he would arrive immediately at a position that it had taken William Woodward Sr. forty years to reach.

Niarchos and Brigadier Scott came over to the United States. In Niarchos' apartment on Sutton Place, I told him he'd have to spend a million, or a million two hundred thousand, if he wanted to get Nashua. He bridled immediately.

"That is ridiculous," he declared. "Tulyar, a champion horse, who has already been in the stud and has proven his ability, has been sold for $750,000."

"That means nothing at all," I said. "Nashua is a real good bet to continue his racing career and become the world's leading money-winner. There are many wealthy Americans who would be most happy to have him."

I went on to point out that his stud value was tremendous. Niarchos just shrugged. On the wall over the mantelpiece in his living room was a magnificent Goya. "That's a Goya, isn't it?" I said.

"Yes," was his response.

"It's worth a fortune," I guessed.

"It is," Niarchos agreed; and that was the only time we agreed on anything.

"Well," I said, "to me it isn't worth $50, because I have no desire for it and no place to put it if I did; but, if I could get Nashua, I'd be willing to beg, borrow or steal any kind of money to get him."

"I wouldn't," he said.

I took another crack at him. "Your best bet, as I told you in the beginning," I argued, "is to buy the lot."

The upshot was that he did come in with a bid. He offered $900,000 for Nashua and let the rest go.

There had been plenty of talk about Nashua, and the broodmares and weanlings, but very little interest had been shown in the horses of racing age (aside from the star) and the yearlings. I was concerned about this and, while doing some thinking early in the morning of the day the bids were to be opened, J. S. Kroese came to my mind.

Jack Kroese, who had raced a stable for many years, had been after me for a long time to find him a couple of nice, reasonably-priced fillies that he could put in the stud after he had raced them. It wouldn't hurt to phone him. So, about eight o'clock in the morning, I phoned his office in downtown Manhattan. He was there.

"Look," I said, "if you buy all the Woodward racehorses and yearlings, I'll guarantee you'll get a couple of fillies that will please you. There is one by Nasrullah, out of Marguery, by Sir Gallahad III, and there's one by Double Jay, out of Rabletta, by Hypnotist II, that I think you'll like. Keep them and put the rest up for auction. You should get your money back and have the fillies as a profit."

"How many are there?" Kroese wanted to know.

I told him there were nine racehorses at Aqueduct and twelve yearlings at Danny Shea's farm in Maryland.

"What are they worth?" he asked.

"I reckon they're worth at least $225,000," I said. "I think you'll get 'em if you come in with a bid of $200,000 plus a few, so as to have an odd figure."

"Okay, I'm a gambler. I'll try it," Jack said. "What do I do now?"

The deadline for bids was 11:00 a.m., so I said, "Meet me at the Hanover Bank, at quarter to eleven with a certified check from your bank for ten per cent of the amount you're going to bid." He said, "Okay," again, and, at 10:45, he met me at the bank, and we wrote out the bid.

Earlier, I had talked to Lou Doherty, who also was interested in the racehorses and yearlings, but he wanted Nashua more than anything. He had thought of bidding on the whole lot, but he had the notion that no one might bid on the horses in training and yearlings, so he put in a bid on them, and one on Nashua.

The bids were opened at the advertised time in the directors' room of the Hanover Bank. Present were a senior partner of Haskins and Sells, accountants; Frank Foley, a partner in the law firm of Dunnington, Bartholow and Miller, counsel to the estate; and myself, president of Fasig-Tipton and technical adviser to the executors. As we had suspected, there were some nutty bids. One fellow sent in a dollar, plus ten cents. There were two bids of $500 and one of $200. Karen Ann McGuire, a twelve-year-old girl who had read about the sale, offered her "life savings" of $24.03 for "any horse that no one will buy," and that story received as much attention in the daily papers as the whole sale.

There were eleven bids on Nashua, five of them over $1,000,000; two on the racehorses and yearlings, two on the mares and foals and one realistic bid on the entire lot. Leslie Combs II, who was in with John W. Hanes and Chris Devine, got Nashua for $1,251,200. Lou Doherty, who had been given liberal backing by William du Pont, Jr., and others, bid $1,226,084, and barely missed. He was tremendously disappointed. A very careful "pencil" man, he had figured that his bid would take the horse. Max Gluck put in a bid of $1,200,000 for Nashua, and as he had no partners, all of it was his own money.

Miss Mildred Woolwine, Kentucky breeder, who had gotten a group together, took the broodmares and foals for $410,000. Larry McPhail was the underbidder with an offer of $351,000. Kroese bid $205,000 for the racehorses and yearlings and that was enough. Lou Doherty bid $201,000. Lou's feeling that perhaps no one else would try for that lot wasn't far wrong, as Kroese's bid was the only other one. Leslie Combs and his group put in a bid of $1,851,200 for everything, but that didn't equal the total of the three separate bids, which added up to $1,866,200. So he didn't miss by much, exactly $15,000.

Parenthetically, and with due modesty, I must mention that my pre-sale estimates were not far off base. I had guessed that Nashua would bring $1,200,000; the racehorses and yearlings, $225,000; the broodmares and foals, $475,000, totaling $1,900,000. The actual selling prices were $1,251,200, $205,000 and $410,000, and a $1,866,200 total.

As soon as Combs was notified that he was the successful bidder on Nashua, he contacted Jim Fitzsimmons, the respected "Mr. Fitz," who agreed to continue training the colt. He had been conditioning the Woodward horses for many years, and he was more than glad to go on with Nashua. Combs then announced that Nashua would be sent to Florida, as soon as convenient, and would be returned to training.

Kroese promptly issued a statement, saying he would sell the horses he purchased—except the two fillies—at Hialeah during the winter. Miss Woolwine and her group also announced that they would resell.

Promptly after the names of the successful bidders were announced, the bank sent out letters notifying all who participated of the outcome. The checks were returned to the unsuccessful bidders.

The Woodward Estate's stallion shares, five in Nasrullah and six in Ambiorix, also were sold by sealed bid. A. B. Hancock and his associates got most of them. Niarchos bought a couple of shares at a tremendous price.

Karen Ann McGuire, the twelve-year-old bidder who offered $24.03 was not disappointed. One hundred and thirty officers of the Hanover Bank, acting as individuals, chipped in and bought her a horse. The day after Christmas I took her to Teddy Wahl's Round Hill Stables in Greenwich, Connecticut. Karen selected an eight-year-old chestnut gelding and named him Hanover's Wishing Star. She was a mighty happy little girl—and she might have been the owner of the only "Hanover" in the country that wasn't a harness horse.

After all the smoke had cleared away from the widely publicized Woodward dispersal, the Internal Revenue Service sent a young man to discuss certain points about my appraisals of the Belair horses at the time of the death of Mr. Woodward, Sr. Mr. Fitz was present when the

IRS representative showed up. The lad couldn't understand the figure I'd put on Nashua in 1953. If, as a four-year-old (which Nashua was on January 1, 1956), the colt was worth $1,251,200, he should have been worth twenty-five per cent of that, or about $300,000, as a one-year-old. It was a matter of simple mathematics. Fitzsimmons just about jumped out of his chair.

"Young man," he barked, "you've got a lot to learn about this business!"

I spelled it out as simply as possible, and told the young investigator what everybody in the horse business knows: nobody can tell by looking at a yearling what his future holds in store. I went back over the appraisal, horse by horse, and showed him some on which I'd put high figures and who'd done no bloody good. The one by Nasrullah, out of Hypnotic, that I priced highest of the lot, had ultimately been sold to somebody in Mexico for $1,500. He'd bowed in both tendons before he ever got to racing. I think that young man did learn something about business that afternoon—the horse business.

In the meantime, immediately after acquiring the twenty-four broodmares and sixteen weanlings, Miss Mildred Woolwine announced that she had engaged Breeders' Sales Company to resell them in the pavilion at Keeneland, on January 6. The sale of Nashua, the other racehorses and yearlings and the shares in stallions had kicked up fantastic interest, and everyone knew that Miss Woolwine's sale was going to be big. Breeders were eager to buy the Nasrullah fillies and the mares in foal to Nasrullah.

I was in Lexington with Marke Zervudachi, secretary to Stavros Niarchos, who had bid on the Belair horses in New York, and had gotten nothing. I had selected five mares from the catalogue, and Niarchos instructed us to buy them. On the first two or three that came up in the morning, I was outbid. Zervudachi was with me, and thought we should have another session with Niarchos. We went to his room, and, for a while, the two of them talked a mile a minute in Greek, while I waited and wondered what it was all about.

When the conference was over, I asked Zervudachi, "What did you get out of all that?"

"We've got to buy some mares," he said.

"What mares?" I asked.

"Why, the mares that you selected," he replied.

"Well, what does he want to pay for them?" I had to know how far he would go.

The answer I got from Zervudachi was not enlightening. He said, "We shall see."

Moon Star II, a Hyperion mare, was among the ones that I had picked out. I thought she was worth about $40,000. She went for $84,000 to Greentree Stud, owned by Jock Whitney and his sister, Mrs. Charles Shipman Payson. They were bidding freely. So was C. V. Whitney. Vagrancy had brought $51,000; Vulcania, $72,000. The prices were much higher than I thought they should be. Hancock bid on three and Vulcania was the only one he got. Sabette went to Bill Helis, Jr. She was Nashua's older sister, and I thought she was a good buy.

I had bid way beyond what I considered the mares were worth and didn't get any of them. Marke was worried.

"We have not done anything," he said. "We have not bought any horses."

"I've bid too much, and I've still been outbid," I said. "I can't see the sense of going overboard,"

"Well," he said, "we must concentrate on Segula."

"What do you mean, 'concentrate'?" I inquired.

"You must buy her," he declared.

Segula was the dam of Nashua, and was in foal to Nashua's sire, Nasrullah, so whatever she produced would be the great horse's full brother or sister. Without a doubt, the mare was coveted by plenty of people with fat bankrolls. I had a pretty thick one backing me, so I said, "All right. Now, I think she's going to make well above $100,000. I'm going to separate the men from the boys. I'm going to start the bidding with $100,000." Such an opening bid never had been made in my time, and I'm damned sure I'm on solid ground when I say that.

When the mare was led into the ring, I tried to attract the attention of the two auctioneers, Doc Bond and George Swinebroad, but they were looking everywhere except where I was. Swinebroad was looking at somebody over on the other side—he had dead aim on whoever it was. Finally, I caught Doc's eye and with my lips shaped the words "A hundred thousand." George paused long enough to make sure, and then said, "I have a bid of $100,000 to start!"

That announcement was followed by what might have been history's most pregnant silence. Many people had been talking about getting together and bidding eighty or a hundred thousand, but this bid knocked them flat out of it. Even George was quiet, and during those noiseless moments, I began to sweat. Had I overshot my mark? Here, I had opened with $100,000 on the first horse I was buying for a man, and nobody else entered the bidding. During those moments of suspense, I wondered, "Could I have gotten it for fifty—or sixty?" There was an excellent chance that I should end up feeling silly, and that Niarchos would be most unhappy about the way I was throwing his money around.

But there's one thing you've got to say for a horse auctioneer; he comes back fast. No matter what is bid, he is ready to assume that somebody else will bid more. Swinebroad was his smooth, persuasive self in seconds—even though it'd seemed like a long time to me—and addressed the person at whom he'd been staring in the first place.

"You told me," George said to the man, "that you were going to pay a lot more money than that for the mare. Now don't let him get away with this. I know him. He's probably got just one bid, and he's shot his bolt."

The man went to $105,000 and I bid $110,000. I saw then that my opponent was Walter Michaels, prominent as an owner of harness horses, and as head of the Bucyrus Erie heavy machinery company. Michaels said $115,000, so I said, "Twenty." Michaels made it $125,-000. I raised my hand, and George looked at me and asked,

"One thirty?"

"No!" I said. "A hundred and twenty-six thousand."

And that was it. I sent Zervudachi to call Niarchos, and get authority to announce the name of the buyer I was representing.

I bought one more mare for Niarchos, Valse d'Or, for $76,000, so I put him in business in America for $101,000 a round (average).

Unfortunately, he had nothing but bad luck with the two mares. Segula produced a filly (Nashua's sister) that had some illness. Named Stavroula, she was sent to England and raced a number of times, but didn't do anything worthy of mention. Segula—the $126,000 mare—never had another foal as long as she lived. She was treated by the best veterinarians in the United States, and then sent to the best in England, but she produced nothing. She died in 1961, a total loss. Valse d'Or had a breach presentation, lost the foal, and died of peritonitis —so she also was a total loss.

As Niarchos was a shipping man, I thought he would be an insurance man, too, and I had covered the mares immediately for the amount paid for them. Niarchos had cut this in half. So, when Valse d'Or died and he lost the mare and foal, he collected only $38,000, when he could have got $76,000.

Looking back on the sale, the best of the lot was Vulcania, which Bull Hancock bought. Miss Woolwine and her associates did very well. The twenty-three mares (of twenty-four purchased) and sixteen yearlings brought a total of $924,100. Where, but in the horse business, can a girl who can scrape up only $410,000 run it to $924,100 in twenty-two days?

After Miss Woolwine had had such a wonderful sale of the stock bought at the Woodward dispersal, the turf world looked forward to the John S. Kroese sale, to see how much of a profit he would rack up. Kroese had bought nine racehorses and twelve yearlings for $205,000 and, like Miss Woolwine, promptly announced that he would sell all the horses except two. He had found it necessary to buy twenty-one horses to get the two fillies he wanted. Those were the ones I had recommended that he keep, the filly by Nasrullah—Marguery, by Sir Gallahad III, and the one by Double Jay—Rabletta, by Hypnotist II.

Kroese, president of the Gaffney-Kroese Electric Supply Company of New York and a major stockholder and a director of Monmouth Park, set January 25 as the date for his sale—the place, Hialeah. As soon as he had bought them, he had sent the racehorses to Florida and kept them in training. The young horses were at Danny Shea's Merryland Farm in Maryland, where interested persons were invited to inspect them.

Nashville, a two-year-old colt, by Nasrullah, out of Bonnie Beryl, brought the biggest price at the sale—$65,000. He was a very good horse. With Charlie Whittingham training, he won $90,895. To his credit is a victory over Bold Ruler as a two-year-old. Later he became a successful sire in California. Mrs. Mary Elizabeth Lunn (now Mrs. CloyceTippett) was Nashville's buyer. Mrs. Lunn also paid $13,500 to get First Flower, a full sister to the Nasrullah filly Kroese kept. Jacnot Stable bought Tremor, a filly by Prince Simon—Vibration, by Sir

Cosmo for $60,000. Black Emperor, a three-year-old by Black Tarquin, went to Hasty House Farm for $20,500.

Kroese's transaction turned out profitably for him, by normal standards, but, coming right on the heels of Miss Woolwine's whopper, it didn't seem like much. The horses brought $301,300. This was $96,300 more than he had paid for them, and he got the two fillies on top of that. The one by Nasrullah—Marguery, was named Marullah and did very well, racing in stakes company, and she was a good producer. The other one didn't do so much. Marguery, incidentally, was Gallant Fox's sister.

NINE

The Aga Khan and Aly

Two people who made a great contribution to the sport of racing were the Aga Khan and his son Prince Aly. Working together, they bred some of the world's greatest horses. The three top sires in America in 1952 were bred by the Aga Khan (with Aly having a finger in the breeding plans). The three horses never will be forgotten by Thoroughbred people. They were Nasrullah, Khaled and Alibhai. From the Khan studs came Noor, Nathoo, Gallant Man, Tulyar, Mahmoud, Blenheim II, Migoli, Poona II, Tehran, Bahram, Owen Tudor, Royal Charger and Umidwar, and countless others. No one in the history of Thoroughbred breeding has produced so many front-ranking horses.

My first dealings with the Aga and his son took place in 1953. That summer the Aga sent over from Ireland four plane loads of horses to be sold at Saratoga. That was the biggest shipment of horses by air ever made up to that time. The cargo consisted of twelve horses of racing age, twenty-four yearlings, and Prince Aly.

The Prince attracted the most attention, by far. For days, before, during, and after the sales, there was a long string of cocktail parties and dinners in his honor. I don't know whether he was present at all of them, because of his other time-consuming interests, but Saratoga's summer colony really laid out the welcome mat for him. The public had not forgotten his romance with Rita Hayworth, and wherever he appeared many eyes followed him. And that wasn't all. When he was moving around the sales area, he usually was followed—at a respectful distance—by females of all ages, from the early teens on up.

Under customs regulations, any alien bringing horses into America must place a valuation on them and pay duty according to that appraisal—about seven per cent—if he sells the horses. Naturally, anybody with horses to sell doesn't wish to put a low rating on them, neither does he care to have the tariff cut deeply into his profits. He is sort of caught in the middle.

Before the 1953 Saratoga sale, the Aga left it to his French manager, Madame Vuillier, to estimate the value of the horses. She did a very flattering job—overvalued them, far and away, on the basis of what she thought the pedigrees would be worth in the sales ring. Some of the fillies of French breeding sold ridiculously low, because the names in the pedigrees meant little or nothing to the buyers. The duties paid were huge in proportion to the prices the horses brought. That is the penalty foreigners must often pay if they sell in our market.

We sold the twelve racehorses in the morning—Saturday, August 14. They brought $159,320, for an average of $13,276.67. Prince Aly thought that was very good. Some of the celebrities who purchased racehorses were radio and TV's Arthur Godfrey, John Hay Whitney, Matt Winn Williamson (grandson of Matt Winn, of Kentucky Derby fame), and Mrs. Mary Elizabeth Person (who was to buy Nashville after she became Mrs. Lunn, and before she became Mrs. Tippett). Prince Aly was her house guest.

The yearlings were put up for sale in the evening, and the bidders just about beat out one another's brains trying to buy anything offered by Aly Khan and his father. The twenty-three that were sold brought $361,700 for an average of $15,726. (One had to be withdrawn.) A half brother to Tulyar, by Tudor Minstrel, went for $75,000 to Miss

Eleonora R. Sears, a septuagenarian who had been a great athlete in her youth, and, incidentally, a great, great granddaughter of Thomas Jefferson.

That was the first of three groups of yearlings the Aga Khan sent over. The second lot was sold, with only slightly less sensational results, at Saratoga in 1954. The third lot, I bought in 1955 for Ralph Lowe, an oilman of Midland, Texas.

The deal whereby Ralph Lowe got Gallant Man came about in the following manner. I was going to Lexington from Baltimore and met Ralph's trainer Willard Proctor on the train. Proc asked me if I knew a good horse deal that would appeal to Ralph Lowe, who was a Midland, Texas oil well driller, and who had some horses and a ranch out in West Texas. I told him I had just received a letter from Major Cyril Hall, the Aga Khan's manager in Ireland, and Cyril had told me that the Aga was prepared to make a deal for the twelve best colts of his entire crop. As I recall it, there were thirty-five or forty colts and something like as many fillies in the crop that year, which was 1955.

I discussed the matter with Ralph and Proctor in Lexington, and found that Lowe was willing to bid on six colts, but would not take more, and was very anxious to get three fillies in addition. They were to be from different good families of the Aga's Stud. We put the proposition to Cyril, who took it up with the Aga. Prince Aly, at that time, was in Venezuela where he had interests in land and horses. They finally agreed to let me come over and see the entire crop of yearlings on the five Irish Studs, which included those from the French Studs as well. I spent several days, about a week in fact, watching them all turned out and just loafing around the paddocks and the stables, observing the colts as they came in and out, their action, etc. I came to the conclusion that there were four outstanding individuals: the brother to Tulyar; a beautiful gray colt by Palestine out of Queen of Bagdad; a handsome son of Royal Charger out of Clovelly; and an Abernant colt out of Cassiope. Another grand looking gray was "spun" by the vet because of a questionable spot in one knee, but a suitable substitute was found; and a handy little bay horse by Migoli, with small and rather doubtful ankles, but a very willing look, was selected to round out the half dozen. I thought he would do very well to keep the pot boiling while the colts with classic potential were being given time to develop.

Having selected the colts, I then turned my attention to the three fillies about which I had no choice. One of them was out of the good producer La Li, but was so crooked I could not consider sending her back to the U.S. After protracted calls to Cannes, where the Aga Khan was staying, he kindly allowed me to substitute a Nearco filly which, while not outstanding, was acceptable. She was subsequently pretty useful and a good producer.

So I had my nine horses all in order, and awaited the arrival of Ralph Lowe's veterinarian. He duly made his inspections, approving all but the little bay colt, whose feet he did not like. They were perfectly sound, tough, and hard looking, but were small and inclined to be narrow. It was my opinion that they would stand training, but the vet would not pass him, so we had to discuss our differences with Ralph, as I was determined the colt should stay in the package. There were no more suitable substitutes in the crop. We tried to telephone Midland from the Curragh, but between the Irish and Texas phone systems we had no success. As neither the vet nor I would budge from our positions, the deal was at that point off, so back to New York we went. On arrival at what was then Idlewild Airport, I telephoned home and explained that the deal we had made with the Aga Khan was that I would select the colts, and the vet would pass them for soundness. As the bay colt's feet were admittedly sound, although not to the vet's liking, under our agreement and European custom Lowe was morally obligated to complete the transaction. Ralph, who prided himself on having conducted his oil business on handshakes rather than contracts for nearly fifty years, asked, "You mean it's a deal?" I said, "Yes, Ralph, it's a deal. I took the horses as your agent and they are bought." "Well," he said, "in that case I'll tell the bank in New York to send you a draft of $220,000." I said, "Thank you very much," and the deal was done.

The horses were shipped over by plane in the next few weeks, and as history shows, they did very well. Tulyar's brother, named Bold Nero, had brilliant speed, and was used in the Belmont Stakes to set a suicidal early pace, killing off Bold Ruler and setting up a new American record for Gallant Man. Royal Clove, the handsome Royal Charger colt, won stakes and sired a few useful horses, as did Aberion, the Abernant colt, who, though plagued by injuries, had real class. The unquestionable star of the group, however, was Gallant Man, the little bay horse who caused the controversy. Second to Iron Liege in the famous Kentucky Derby in which Shoemaker mistook the sixteenth pole for the finish marker, Gallant Man won the Belmont Stakes and many other good races, and earned over $500,000 for home under the tutelage of Hall of Fame trainer Johnny Nerud. Ralph subsequently sold three-quarters of him for stud duty for $1,000,000, and Gallant Man has been among the leading sires for the past decade. It is worthy of note that in 1973 the little horse looks just the same out at Spendthrift Farm, and his feet, regardless of their shape, are as sound as they were on the Curragh in 1955.

Prince Aly's knowledge of horses and his memory for particulars was incredible. After one of my trips to the Newmarket December Sales, I went over to France with him to see the horses Alec Head was training for him at Chantilly. I was amazed at the amount of information Aly carried in his head. We stood in the center of a circle while thirty-five yearlings—soon to be two-year-olds—galloped slowly around us. Aly could name every one of them and give particulars regarding the breeding. One was Eblouissante, a filly I had picked up for him at Saratoga. She was by Bolero, out of Graciously, by Sir Gallahad III. She became a stakes winner in France. Later, I repurchased her as a broodmare from the Aga Khan for her breeders, Mrs. Charles Ferguson and her son, Ben, of Paris, Kentucky. Aly pointed out Eblouissante, and remembered everything about her. And that's the way it was with the whole thirty-five. He knew them all, and all about their relatives—what their brothers and sisters had done—and how their dams had performed on the course and in production. I took particular pains to notice the markings on some of them—just to check him out. He didn't make a mistake; nobody has a right to be *that* good.

Before his death in May 1960, Prince Aly conceived the idea that a sale of art treasures in the Canfield Casino might add an interesting attraction to Saratoga Springs night life. Aly had the notion that, after the week of the sales was over, some vacationers just didn't know what to do with themselves at night, though I do not think he was numbered in that group. Mrs. Jere Field, an art dealer in Paris, agreed to put on the show. She came over and brought with her fifty-four paintings worth a quarter of a million dollars—the newspapers said. Some were Mrs. Field's property; a few were on consignment, with reserve prices attached.

This was no ordinary stuff. There were works by Renoir, Picasso, Cézanne, Rouault, Vuillard, Dufy, Bonnard, Vlaminck and others, all painters of the late nineteenth century or the twentieth. The pictures were on exhibition for three days and attracted about 300 lookers a day. The Chamber of Commerce gave full cooperation, and the affair created quite a stir. It was held on the evening of Monday, August 15. John and I did the auctioneering, calling attention to conformation and genesis of each painting and giving our best pitch.

George Murphy, writing in the Albany *Times-Union*, had predicted that: "Pierre Auguste Renoir will have to go some to beat Nashua." By that he meant that Renoir's "Portrait du Jeune Halphen en Costume de Marin" wasn't going to bring $1,251,200, no matter how long, how loud and how persuasively John and I hollered. It was a very sound prediction. Art connoisseurs had estimated the value of the painting at $25,000.

Jere supplied us with the name of each subject, the artist and background material. John and I alternated in selling in the English style—talking quietly to the people and selling directly to them. I would sell a picture while John boned up on the next one, and then he'd sell one while I got ready for my turn. Each painting was displayed on an easel. It was like having a horse in the ring, and Canfield's Casino seemed an appropriate place for an art gamble.

The catalogue did not give the complete pedigree of the artist, nor the prices brought by other creations of his brush. In a word, very little in the way of past performances was available. The headline in the New York *Times* the day after the auction, gave a rather harsh, but honest description of the sale. It said: "Famous Paintings Left at the Post at Saratoga."

Though the exhibition had attracted something close to 1,000 window shoppers in three days, only about 200 breathing mortals showed up for the sale. Over a million dollars was bet at the races in the afternoon, and $2,726,200 had been spent on yearlings the week before, but all we could get for the priceless pictures was $91,900. A substantial part of that was for "buy ins," items that didn't reach their reserves and were taken back by the consignors. The Renoir valued at $25,000 was listed as sold for $12,000, but it was bought back by its original owner, as were several other valuable paintings.

There were plenty of legitimate sales, though. An aquarelle of a horse with a groom, by Raoul Dufy, brought $5,000. That picture went to Joseph Kriegler, who came over from Buffalo expressly to buy it. But, all in all, it was, as we say at Fasig-Tipton, "a buyer's market." No plans were made for a subsequent sale.

On May 12, 1960, Prince Aly Khan died in Paris, after a crackup in his sports car. Whatever his image was to the world, he was kind to those around him and a man of great intelligence. His father had showed his confidence in Aly when he made him a full partner in his Thoroughbred operations and placed him in charge of his stud farms and racing interests in Ireland and France. Aly expanded his own horse interests and, at the time of his death, had six farms—two in Ireland and four in France. The best known, of course, was Sheshoon in Eire.

Aly was raised with horses and rode as a gentleman jockey in the '30s. From his allowance of $3,000 a year, he saved enough to buy a horse named Sledge, his first racehorse. He sold Sledge at a big profit and said later, "From the money I made on Sledge, I formed my own stable." He still worked closely with the Aga, who had learned to respect the young man's judgment about horses. While in his early twenties, Aly spent $115,000 in one day, buying horses for his father.

"The Aga knew nothing about conformation," Aly often said. "I could have sold him a horse with knock-knees if the bloodlines were impressive."

Having unlimited capital never hurt anyone in the horse business, but that wasn't the whole story. The Aga's determination to have only the very best bloodlines and Aly's keenness regarding physical correctness combined to make the enterprise a tremendous success.

Every mating was planned carefully. "I've never owned a chance-bred horse," Aly once said. For every one of the multitude of mares under his direction, he chose what he considered exactly the right sire. Also, he insisted that he was in business to make a profit, and that he never regretted letting a good horse get away from him. "As a seller," he said, "I will always be interested in selling good horses. I want the people who buy them to return and buy some more. A good horse is the best advertisement for our bloodstock." Aly's passing was a loss to the world of racing.

Nashua, Eddie Arcaro up, training at old Aqueduct Race Track. New York, 1955. *Photo courtesy Bert and Richard Morgan Studio.*

Prince Aly Khan has a hard time with the crowds. Saratoga, 1953. *Photo courtesy Bert and Richard Morgan Studio.*

Last sale together for Swinebroad and Finney. Pomona, California, January 1959.

Captain Harry Guggenheim and H.S.F. Keeneland, 1965. *Photo courtesy John C. Wyatt.*

Crowned Prince, son of Raise a Native and Gay Hostess, by Mahmoud, and the finest specimen of Thoroughbred yearling I have seen in a sales ring. He has a classic head, a beautiful front, excellent, sloping shoulders. He stands on four well-placed legs, with plenty of bone and good, big feet, and is an excellent mover. Well ribbed-up, with a short coupling, he has a good body and loin. The look of eagles is in his eye. The highest priced yearling up to 1973, he made $510,000 and went to England to race. There, at two, he won the prestigious Champagne and Dewhurst Stakes and was winter favorite for the English Classics. A wind problem stopped him at three and he was syndicated for $1,200,000. *Photo courtesy Tony Leonard.*

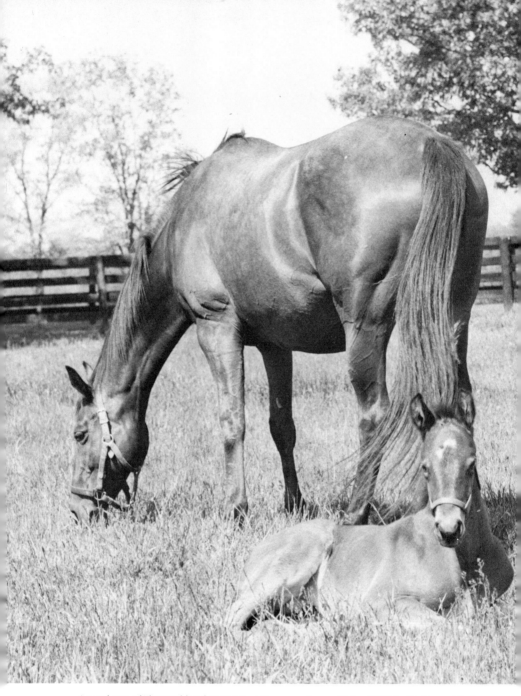

A good type of Thoroughbred mare is Fast Turn, seen here with her 1973 foal in the paddock. *Photo courtesy* The Thoroughbred Record.

Humphrey Finney with grandson Michael Humphrey Stanley Finney. Saratoga, 1968. *Photo courtesy Peter Winants.*

Tattersalls' new sales pavilion, at Park Paddocks, Newmarket, with the historic "Fox" on the right. *Photo courtesy John Slater Photography Ltd. Newmarket.*

Would-be jockeys are taught jumping during their training at Japan Racing Association's Equestrian Park, outside Tokyo.

The Finneys, Humphrey and John, study the Summer Sales catalogue. Keeneland, 1967. *Photo courtesy* The Thoroughbred Record.

Your Host at Meadowview Farm with groom Frank Burrell. Moorestown, New Jersey, 1960.
Photo by Allen F. Brewer, Jr.

Will Harbut with Man o' War, the "Mostest Hoss," at Faraway Farm, Lexington. *Photo by J. C. Skeets Meadors.*

A great pair, B.A. (Plain Ben) and H.A. (Jimmie) Jones, Calumet Farm's inimitable trainers. *Photo courtesy* The Thoroughbred Record.

The Humphrey S. Finney Pavilion. Saratoga, 1968. *Photo courtesy Bert and Richard Morgan Studio.*

Inside the Humphrey S. Finney Pavilion. Saratoga, 1969. *Photo courtesy Peter Winants.*

At dinner given by the Saratoga Chamber of Commerce honoring Fasig-Tipton. President Tom Ashton presents H.S.F. with a gavel made from a balustrade rail from the defunct Grand Union Hotel. Saratoga, 1959.

The Finneys at home, under the watchful eye of Grandfather Rev. William Henry Finney, the first. Verasilles, Kentucky, 1970. *Photo by Heinrich von Michaelis.*

SECRETARIAT
1973

Michaelis

Triple-crown winner Secretariat, one of America's all-time greatest racehorses, combines superb conformation, an ideal constitution and a lovely disposition with outstanding ability. He can run "short" or "long," on dirt or turf, in mud or on a fast track. This is the beau ideal that every breeder hopes to produce. *From the painting by Heinrich von Michaelis, done after the Belmont Stakes, 1973.*

TEN

Buying
for other People

Though I have planned hundreds of matings and bought hundreds of horses, I never have bred a horse for myself, nor owned one that set a foot on a racetrack. During the years when I was field secretary of the Maryland Horse Breeders Association, there was an unwritten law that I should not be in competition with my employers, the breeders. With Fasig-Tipton, also, I followed this policy. But I have often bought horses for others.

As a regular buyer at Keeneland, I had the same seats at the sales there from the end of World War II until 1969, when the new pavilion was built. Then, I was invited to choose seats that would be mine permanently—with my name on them, as it had been on the others. I chose a location in the second row, well over on the right side facing the ring. From that position, a horse is coming toward me as it enters the ring, and I can observe its action. I see it head on and then broadside—and get a look at all four legs. Of course, if you expect to spend a lot of money for a horse, you're going to look it over from top to bottom before it goes on the block; but, if you're seated right and look them over as they come in, you might notice something that appeals to you and pick up a bargain.

Years ago, I used to buy cheap horses for Ray Bryson—maybe half a dozen a year—when well-bred fillies could be bought for $2,500 or $3,000. Some of them I didn't know anything about, except what was in the catalogue. If I liked them when they came into the ring, I bid on them. In many instances, though, I saw defects that caused me to stay out of the auction. I picked up several useful fillies for Gee Cohen and Stanley Sagner, of Maryland, just by watching horses led into the ring, and buying the ones that had the right look.

Frequently, people have called me at the last minute and said, "Buy such-and-such a horse for me—if you like it." Maybe I haven't even seen the horse, but if I'm seated right, and look it over carefully as it walks, I can get some idea of the kind of creature it is. Possibly, the main point is a negative one. If the factors presented in the catalogue are satisfactory, the decision to buy or not to buy has to be made on the conformation and physical condition of the horse. One look might convince me that I *don't* want to buy. Some are quickly eliminated from consideration. You can cut 'em down right quick.

I was at Hialeah, in February 1957, when a horse named Nirfren won an allowance with a gross value of $7,500—nothing sensational, but Nirfren was an old friend. Back in 1955, a man had called me and asked, "Do you buy horses for people?" I admitted that I had been known to do so on occasion.

"I have $1,600," the man said, "and I want to buy a horse."

"Are you a horseman?" I inquired.

"No," he said, "I play the flute with the D'Oyly Carte Opera Company." I had to think about that a minute.

"Let's see now," I said. "You're a Gilbert and Sullivan flute player, and you have $1,600, and you want to buy a horse? Do you have any idea of what it costs to train a horse? You know buying a horse is like buying a marriage license. The initial cost is nothing compared with the upkeep. Now why don't you take your $1,600 . . ."

He interrupted before I could recommend a relatively painless way to get rid of $1,600. "Let me come and see you anyhow," the man said, and he did. He was quiet, polite and firm. He definitely wanted a horse. "I have a trainer friend who will go easy on me," he said. He added that he might be able to scrape up as much as $2,000.

When I got to the Keeneland Fall Sales, I remembered about the flutist. I looked over every horse that went through the ring. There were sons and daughters of Alibhai, Citation, Nasrullah and Heliopolis, but there weren't any $2,000 ones. Everyday, the flute player called my office in New York and asked, "Has Mr. Finney bought me a horse yet?" After this had been going on for days, I sent back the word that he'd have to rustle up another $1,000. He got a partner, a trombone player, who had enough to make their total $3,000.

At that time, John W. Galbreath was selling off some yearlings. With a big operation like his, cutting down periodically is part of the routine. Sometimes, a good horse can be picked up at such a sale. Nobody knows what's inside a horse until he shows you.

From Mr. Galbreath, I picked up a nice little fellow by Nirgal—Friendly, by Blenheim II. I got him for $2,600. The owners were ecstatic. Red Smith, in his *Herald-Tribune* column, described them as "the happiest flutist and trombone player this side of La Scala."

The colt was put into the hands of John (Trader) Clark, in Lexington, to be broken. Clark took a liking to Nirfren, as the young Thoroughbred had been named, and started training him for the races. When John got the colt ready for his first race, the owners couldn't have been held down by wires. They were wild. The D'Oyly Carte players quit New York for the road, so the trombonist and flute player quit the D'Oyly Carte Opera Company. They signed up with the orchestra that was playing for "My Fair Lady," so they could remain near their horse. Devotees of betting sometimes show indications of mild insanity, but horse owners, particularly first-time starters, go further.

These two did all right. They won a couple of races, and then the colt was claimed away from them for $7,500. I have the album from "My Fair Lady," and there is a place where the flute goes soaring off by itself. When I play the record and hear that joyous flute player tearing off those trills, I say, "Here comes Nirfren, making his move in the stretch."

I don't know what happened to the two musicians, but Nirfren did well enough, and he went to stud at Redbob Farms, Oxford, Michigan. His stud fee, when I last heard, was $350. But money isn't everything.

John Olin is the man who built the Olin-Matheson Corporation. Also, he operates an experimental game farm, Nilo Farms, near his home in Alton, Illinois. Many horsefolk have hunted ducks, quail and pheasant on this wide-ranging acreage. At one time, Olin showed three- and five-gaited horses with Mrs. Olin, but they tired, he said, "of those judges." In 1960, he disposed of his show horses and started buying Thoroughbreds. He paid $75,000 for a son of Nashua at Keeneland and named it Nasholin.

At Keeneland, in '61, Olin fell in love with a perfectly splendid chestnut son of Swaps, out of Obedient, a gray mare, by Mahmoud. She had produced Don't Alibi, Obey, and Blazing Count, so everybody was aware that the colt—in the consignment of Leslie Combs II— wasn't going for peanuts.

Olin asked me what I thought the animal would bring. I said "About $95,000, or maybe a hundred."

He said, "Buy him for me."

"For how much?" I asked.

"As high as necessary to get him," Olin replied. "You have an open order."

I like a man like that, even when my company doesn't get the five per cent.

With the combination of desirable breeding and excellent conformation, the Swaps colt was coveted by many. Almost before you could find the page in the catalogue, the bidding was up to $95,000. Then, somebody offered $100,000. I was getting a little itchy, so I looked over at Mr. Olin; he looked away, but he gave me the thumbs-up sign. I bid $105,000. There were two or three more bids, but the action paused when R. F. Bensinger, of Chicago, said, "One, twenty-six." George Swinebroad looked at me with his gavel poised. I said, "Thirty." That ended it; George banged his gavel and Mr. Olin had his horse.

To that time, that was the highest-priced yearling Thoroughbred sold in the history of public auctions. Olin was pleased and proud. Later, he said, "When you see an animal like this one and you set your heart on it, you can't let ten or fifteen thousand dollars stop you." The colt was given the name of Swapson and was a pretty decent runner, but he didn't win $130,000, by a jugful.

Andre Rueff, a Swiss banker living in Paris, had what many turf enthusiasts would consider the ideal place of residence. He could sit at his window and watch the races. Because he wanted to buy some American-bred horses to race in France, I conferred with him at Auteuil, while on my 1961 European trip. We watched a race or two at the course, and then repaired to his flat and witnessed the rest of the card. The next morning, we went to Chantilly to see Mr. Rueff's horses. In conversations during the hours we were together, he described what he was looking for and gave me an order to buy four horses. That was the beginning of an interesting and pleasant association. Each year, thenceforth, until Mr. Rueff died, I bought about four yearlings for him in America—ranging between $15,000-$20,000 in price—and shipped them to France. Practically all of the American yearlings we sent over were winners, and one of them, a colt by Noor named Yours, was a first-class sprinter in France and has sired a number of useful runners.

A number of people ask me to buy horses for them as Mr. Rueff did. In this work, I follow a regular routine. I find out, as nearly as possible, what the client has in mind—how much he is willing to spend, whether he wants a horse for sprinting or staying, and whether he wants fillies. Some people don't care to have any fillies at all; others would like a filly or two. The ultimate in the sport is breeding your own, and you have to have females if you plan to do that. Those who want fillies, naturally, want attractive pedigrees.

When I get an open order, I record it with the office, so that others besides myself are aware that this particular type of horse is wanted. I like to have plenty of time. If you are rushed, and in too much of a hurry, you're likely to have to pay fancy prices. Taking your time, you're able to shop around during the year, and, when the opportunity arises, pick up the kind of horse the man wants at a reasonable price.

I might even see something in one of our own sales that is just what my man is looking for, and I'll throw in a bid or two. Of course,

Fasig-Tipton doesn't charge the buyer a commission if the horse is bought out of our sale. If we buy an animal privately, or at a sale staged by another company, we make a charge. If it is bought at our sale, the Company's commission comes from the vendor.

Early in August 1969, John W. Gaines, of Gainesway Farm, Lexington, Kentucky, phoned and suggested that I call Lady Beaverbrook in London, as she was interested in buying some colts by Ribot. Mr. Gaines had published a very handsome catalogue describing in word and picture his offerings at the Saratoga Sales and had sent a copy to Lady Beaverbrook. In it she saw a Ribot colt that struck her fancy, so she wrote to Gaines inquiring about it. He cabled her, suggesting that she get in touch with me. Then she cabled him asking him to tell me to call her up.

There was a lot of back-and-forth stuff before I finally got the message. Lady Beaverbrook had had dealings with the British Bloodstock Agency, Fasig-Tipton's associate in England, and knew our company. Also, Sir Gordon Richards, her trainer, and I had been friends for many years. I met him when he first started training, before he took over the English string of Canadian E. P. Taylor.

Before I made my call, I looked over the Ribots in the sale, and did not care to recommend them. One I rejected on pedigree, the other on his physical make-up. Lady Beaverbrook was hoping to get a classic colt and the one I passed up on breeding was just about halfway there. I didn't think he was up to what the client wanted. The other was not a bad specimen, but could be faulted and was somewhat nervous. I explained these things to Lady Beaverbrook and she said, "If you can't get a Ribot, do you think you could get me a Sea-Bird?"

"I haven't looked at them," I told her, "but I will."

There were two colts and a filly, and she didn't want a filly. One of the colts was bred by Danny Van Clief, at Nydrie Stud in Virginia, and it was out of Right of the Line, a good mare that Danny had raced with some success in England. The young horse was a most attractive bay, very straight and sound, from a family that Lady Beaverbrook knew well. The other was a chestnut out of Rudoma, consigned by Mrs. Harry A. Love of Maryland. I liked that one, too, but was most attracted to the bay.

I reported back, and Lady Beaverbrook asked, "How much do you think the Van Clief colt will bring?" At that time, Sea-Birds had been going for fantastic prices, so I told her I thought it would bring $100,000 or more—possibly $150,000. It depended upon how many people wanted it. If two or three or more were interested, there was no telling where the bidding might go. "In my opinion," I said, "it won't go for less than $100,000."

"Bid $125,000," she said, "but you have a little leeway. Have it vetted and, if it's all right, go ahead."

Shortly after Dr. William O. Reed had completed a thorough examination of the colts, I received a phone call from Sir Gordon Richards.

"Don't forget," the trainer reminded me, "you have a little leeway. If you can't get the one you like best for $125,000, you have a little leeway. Don't get short for a little," he added. "She wants the 'orse. She wants the 'orse."

Then I received a call from Lady Beaverbrook. She asked, "At what time will this horse be sold?" She was speaking of the colt out of Right of the Line.

"About nine o'clock, or nine-fifteen," I estimated.

"Will you call me right away?" she requested.

"Lady Beaverbrook," I said, "that will be in the small hours of the morning, Greenwich Time."

"No matter," she responded. "Call me."

I took a seat in the balcony before the colt came into the ring, so I could watch the bidding and see *who* was bidding. I could see who they were, but they couldn't see me. Jeremy Tree, Jock Whitney's English trainer, was over on one side and Vincent O'Brien, who trained for Charles Engelhard in Ireland, was on the other—and I was looking down on them. It didn't take long to find that this horse wasn't going to be bought for $125,000, and I began to wonder about the literal definition of "a little leeway," in Lady Beaverbrook's lexicon.

I know now. It's no less than $50,000, because that's how much I had to dip into the "leeway" to get the colt. When I bid $175,000, that was it. I went straight to the telephone, and called Lady Beaverbrook. She was waiting to hear from me. I told her I had bought the horse and how much I had to pay.

She said, "Wonderful! How soon can you get him here?"

"When would you like to have him?" I asked.

"Tomorrow!" was her surprising response.

I explained that getting a shipping permit and Government tests would take a day or two. A check must be made for glanders, a contagious disease that is communicable to man. A horse so infected is not allowed to go into England. The owner's vet makes the test, and the Government vet reads it.

I had bought the bay Sea-Bird colt on Thursday night. On Friday, I went after the chestnut, out of Rudoma, which had been a pretty good racemare, but her pedigree wasn't quite up to that of the other colt's dam. I expected he'd bring about $75,000. Mackenzie Miller was bidding for Charles Engelhard, who had left the sales ring. When the price got up to $75,000, I began to wonder how far Engelhard would want to go; but I put in one more bid, $80,000, and got the horse. I think that Miller might have gone on if Engelhard had been there. There's nothing like having the owner at your side when you're bidding for him. You know when to turn it on or turn it off.

We shipped the two horses out of New York, by plane on Monday; they were unloaded in England on Tuesday, and Lady Beaverbrook had her first look at them on Wednesday. She was delighted. "I'm thrilled," she told me over the phone. "Everyone is coming to look at them. They're the cynosure of all eyes." I was glad I had taken advantage of the "leeway," but the thought that came to my mind was: "All they have to do now is run a little."

Sir Gordon Richards took them over, and got the Sea-Bird—Right of the Line colt to the races in June 1970. Lady Beaverbrook had named him Seaepic. His first start was in the Soltykoff Stakes. Jockey Edward Hide sent him to the front at the break and he won by four lengths. His performance impressed *Sporting Life*'s reporter who said: "Seaepic has a bright future. The manner of his success suggests there will be plenty more to come. If he wins his other two scheduled starts of the year, the Richmond Stakes and the Middle Park, Seaepic will not look expensive at such a price."

Seaepic won another race, to the delight of Lady Beaverbrook, and was "put by" to wait for the next season. He did not ultimately fulfill his promise owing to physical problems, but he did give his owner some moments of real satisfaction.

I suppose $175,000 wasn't too big a price to pay—for Lady Beaverbrook.

ELEVEN

On Selling Horses

The process of evolution never ceases, and this is as true of horse trading as of anything else. There always is something new to learn in the horse business, if you are observant. If you are not willing to learn and accept new ideas and new methods, you might as well lie down and let them put the flowers on your chest.

I witnessed my first auction in 1917 at Eaton Hall, in Cheshire, England, and was terribly impressed by the top hats and tails. The auctioneers dressed as though they were about to enter the Royal Enclosure at Ascot. Later, I went to the Newmarket December Sales. There, they sold seven or eight hundred head from Monday to Friday, with five auctioneers working in turns from 9:00 a.m. to about seven in the evening. Buyers came from all over the world. I decided then that this was a very wonderful business. No matter what the horses brought, the sales company got five per cent, and there was always a buyer for everything. I'm sure it didn't occur to me that, in a few decades, I would be deep in the horse-selling business.

I am convinced that the best way to sell horses is through public auction. The sales organization is already set up, and the horses offered for sale provide items of news that appear in the racing dailies and breeders' magazines. A man trying to sell horses from his farm talks to one prospect at a time. The auctioneer pits one bidder against another. Selling from home, the horse farmer must keep his stock slicked up and ready for inspection at any time, if he hopes to get his price. The "pressure period" is much shorter if the sale is at a definite date and approximate hour.

In my business, we live from sale to sale. We put on from twenty-five to thirty sales a year which total a hundred or more sessions of selling. While we are finishing one, we are preparing for another, and every new one presents a challenge—to get what the horses are worth. At times, buyers go wild and all kinds of extravagant prices are paid. But then there will be sales when nobody seems to have any money— or, when whoever has it is keeping it. The mood can often be felt before the sale. Sometimes, the atmosphere will be charged and you know that there's going to be a great sale. Another time, something will just tell you that you're going to have to work hard to get your prices.

For the consignor, having a horse in a sale is similar to having one in a race. Like a racehorse owner, he can be delightfully surprised or dreadfully disappointed. The difference is that the racehorse owner will have another chance on another day. The horse seller has one shot, and that's it!

We who conduct the sales invade the field of histrionics, in our own not-completely-subtle way. We ham it up a little. We enjoy getting laughs and contriving to pit one buyer against another, and many of the attitudes and artifices of the stage are used to cajole the customers and keep them in a generous frame of mind. Even the spotters, who stand in the aisles and look for buying signals that might be missed by the auctioneer and announcer, have their moments. The beckoning gesture, the shrug and the naively hopeful look are used, along with a wide repertoire of facial expressions that range from open admiration to unadulterated contempt. These devices are used also by the announcer and auctioneer, but with finer nuances. Every sale is a new show.

But, at the same time, of course, one must always remember that to build credibility you have to refrain from over-selling or stretching a point too far. As Louie Mayer taught me years ago, while you must give full attention to everything, you shouldn't waste time on the horses that obviously aren't going to bring much money; emphasize the really good ones and take the time on them, not on the mediocre ones. Another thing, of course, is that when you are on the auction stand it is very important to know who you are selling to. If you are familiar with the business, you pretty much know who your buyers are and what their tastes are and how much they like to spend on an animal —and you will also know how to approach them.

When you have a sale to operate, you consider first the promotion and advertising that it will need and should be able to justify in return. Basically, we figure that about one-half of one per cent of the expected gross of the sale should be spent on advertising. It is necessary to build up interest and excitement about the arrangements especially when a big sale of important animals is planned. But the first thing you have to do is to make it clear when the sale will be held, where it will be held, and what will be offered. That governs the amount of advertising space that will be required.

It is not necessary to over-advertise as so many people do, particularly when the animals being offered don't really have the appeal to justify the expense. Whenever photographs are used, they must be good ones that will make the animals look good; otherwise it is better not to use them at all. It is much better to advertise with just plain type than to have a photograph that is improperly taken and does not do the animal justice.

Different sales require different treatments. When Fasig-Tipton put on the Widener sale at the Kentucky Training Center, there were a small number of animals to be offered in a very difficult area to reach by public transportation and to make matters worse, the sale was to be held in the dead of winter. Arrangements were made to charter a Delta Airlines DC-9 jet to bring potential bidders from Miami to Lexington, arriving early enough for people to have time to look at the horses and attend the sale, and returning to Miami as soon as the sale was over. It was an expensive piece of promotion, with the cost shared by the consignor, but it was well worthwhile, as the passengers invested over two million dollars at the sale, and were underbidders on animals which sold for another million. The charter technique was first utilized by Fasig-Tipton in 1966, when the du Pont Sale was held at Timonium, also in the middle of the winter. In that instance, planes from Lexington and Miami arrived the day before the sale. Entertainment was provided for the prospective buyers and no detail was overlooked to insure their comfort and convenience. It was expensive, but like the Keiffer sale, the customers showed their appreciation by emptying their pockets.

The setting up and operation of a Thoroughbred auction is essentially a matter of experience. It looks very simple to people who just watch, but, believe me, it isn't. First of all, the sales setting itself is important. You want to have the most possible available room. But you don't want the area to be too big because, if you're in the auction stand, you like to be able to talk to people, to be able to look them straight in the eye at the shortest possible distance. The trouble with our big pavilion in Kentucky, for instance, is that we're too far away from the floor and we have to depend on a bid spotter—an alert man who will cover a certain section of the house. Otherwise, if a man puts up his arm to bid and he's, say, 200 feet from the auctioneer, he may not be seen.

A good auctioneer has good presence, a good voice, and confidence. He has a big job. The announcer can be of great help to the auctioneer, or he can be just somebody sitting there reading out of the book. He does give the auctioneer a break—just by doing some of the necessary talking. Normally, if we have a sale of fifty or sixty horses, we will have two auctioneers and each one will sell half. You'll sometimes see others do it, but we never sell more than twenty-five or thirty without a break. Particularly when the weather's hot or there's a lot of pressure on the auctioneer.

The most important thing for the auctioneer is to know the horses. I've found it helps a great deal to have many years' experience studying pedigrees and the families. Then you really have something to say. You've got to know the value of what you're selling. The trouble with too many auctioneers is that they're not horsemen, so they don't know what they're selling. Furthermore, a lot of them are trained in that confounded tobacco chant. The theory of the chant is that the voice lasts longer. That's the theory—but if I had my choice I'd abolish it.

In my day, we would sit down with the consignor and attempt to estimate what the horse would bring. If the owner wished to put a "reserve" on the animal, we would start the bidding ourselves with perhaps a half of that amount. If I thought a horse was going to bring $100,000, say, I would start him at twenty-five or fifty thousand myself, because I knew damn well somebody was going to bid higher. I hate to see a horse that is likely to bring a big price go dragging along from $5,000 to $11,000 to $13,000 and on and on.

When we sell, we catalogue the offerings alphabetically by the dam and we skip five letters a year. So, we'll start off selling those beginning with 'A' one year, and the following we'll start with the 'G's. It's absolutely fair, and that way nobody can get annoyed at you for putting his horse first or last in line.

Another policy we have instituted is to tape all auctions. One year, right after we had begun this practice, Harry M. Warner accused us of having sold him a horse from a Mayer sale which had tied up (had had kidney trouble) but which we had pronounced sound. Here is where the tapes came in handy.

We set up a session with Mr. Warner's lawyers, and it was quite a meeting. Attorney Neil S. McCarthy and I sat on one side of the table and three attorneys representing Mr. Warner sat on the other. The tape was played. First came the routine speech at the beginning of the sale which says there are no guarantees of soundness, other than certain ones mentioned. Then, the announcement describing the filly was played. "This animal tied up prior to Christmas," the tape reported, "but was let up on and has had no trouble since." The recording of the actual bidding and the sale followed. Mr. Warner's lawyers looked at one another, and then said to McCarthy, "Thank you very much." The question was answered and the case was closed.

After that, Fasig-Tipton improved on the recording technique and added videotapes, so now when the announcer talks, you see him as well as hear him. This is one of the many innovations the company has added to guarantee the integrity of the sales.

By tradition, the big yearling sales have been held in July and August, but shaking off the bonds of tradition has become a popular practice in recent years. Now a one-year-old can be brought in almost any month of the year. Many sales, besides the ones in July at Lexington and in August at Saratoga, are offering young horses of classic breeding. Also flying in the face of tradition are breeders who sell their young stock as weanlings, late in autumn, instead of holding them over until the next season. A good foal will sell as high as a yearling nowadays.

Sales of two-year-olds in training have also become popular. The Hialeah Sale of juveniles quickly developed into a winter institution. Many topflighters have gone through the ring there. Roman Brother is one that comes to mind. He sold for $23,500, and earned $943,473, and was Horse of the Year. Holding a horse until it is two and getting it ready to race adds greatly to the breeder's expenses, but Florida producers feel that they are getting prices which more than pay the added effort and cost.

Unless a man is prepared to spend $200,000 or more—perhaps much more—the only way to acquire a stakes horse is to buy it before it is one. A horseman is not likely to sell a champion, after he has developed it, except at a price that would be a fortune to most people. At the same time, a breeder who consigns his young horses to sales is wise if he nominates them to stakes events—one or two anyway. This shows confidence in the future of the animal and makes it more desirable from the buyer's point of view. Hence, a better price.

Opinions, pro and con, on the use of the reserve bid, have been expressed by thoughtful people. For my part, I don't see why anyone should give away his horse. If a breeder sets a minimum price, I see no reason why he should accept a lower bid. At the same time, he should be sure the figure he had fixed upon is realistic.

No matter how rosy the dreams of the breeder may be, a horse is worth only what you can get for him. After the 1958 Garden State yearling sale, the worst in its five-year history, some sad sacks were sitting around thinking that this was the end of everything. I explained that there was no reason for the Jersey breeders to go home and humanely destroy all their broodmares (though a good culling out wouldn't have hurt).

"They brought what they were worth," is a fact I tried to emphasize. It has been true all through the years I have been selling and buying horses. There have been sales at which middling horses brought fantastic prices, and times when the prices on good stock were disappointing, but usually, there has been an explanation. One or two well-heeled eager buyers can affect a sale favorably, and a dozen different reasons can cause prices to fall under the pre-sale estimates. A highly successful dispersal of first-rate horses a few days earlier can hurt a sale. Buyers are pulling in their horns. They've got what they wanted and, possibly, spent more money than they had intended to. They're not interested in buying again so soon. At the time of the Jersey sale mentioned, horse production had caught up with and passed demand, so it was a buyer's market and buyers could afford to be discriminating.

The beginning of preparation for the sale of a horse is really the beginning of raising the horse. If horses are properly taken care of, handled, looked after, they don't need much additional preparation for sales. It is true that some breeders may start preparing their yearlings for sale by putting them in separate paddocks. The paddocks should be plenty big enough for them to have adequate exercise. Keep the horses as close to nature as you possibly can. Of course, you have been taking care of their feet, keeping them trimmed, and in proper balance each month throughout their lives, so the feet should be in good order.

The one thing you can pay more attention to closer to sales time is handling. Horses should be taught to walk properly straight out with purpose and a good style. One of the very few men who really does that to perfection is Robin Scully's stud manager at Clovelly, Lars LaCour. Lars is an energetic man himself, and insists on having energetic yearlings. He teaches his men to lead the horses with a free rein and at least a foot of the shank free. The men walk straight forward and then back again. The yearlings are followed in the initial stages by encouragement from the rear, perhaps a snapping whip or something of that sort. But the point is that it makes all the difference in the world when a yearling is brought out to show to prospective buyers if he walks straight away like a horse who knows his business and knows where he is going.

Whether a yearling is on its home farm, or in its stall at the site of the sale, interested persons will want it brought out where they can see it. Consignors should train their men to show off the horses to best advantage. I've seen yearlings put in a position like an elephant on a tub. Such things cause me considerable concern. After all, I own five per cent of that animal, and I want him to look like a $50,000 horse. The consignor should feel the same way, and should take pains to see that the horse's best points are brought out in the way it is posed. If the horse has any weaknesses—heaven forbid—skillful handling can make them less obvious.

When I was in France in December 1957, I went out to Beauvais to look over some weanlings a man named Cruz-Valer wanted to sell to Larry MacPhail. They were the wildest bunch of foals I ever saw. They never had had halters on them, and they couldn't be made to stand so I could have a look at them. I bought none. To my mind, there is nothing more annoying to a prospective buyer than to have horses scrambling all over the place when he is trying to see what they look like. I had traveled sixty or seventy miles out in the country on an absolutely fruitless chase. Those horses might have been the best-looking ones in France, but I'll never know. Jumping around like grasshoppers as they were, it was impossible to get any kind of an idea as to how they were put together. That's why I always emphasize the importance of the proper presentation of a for-sale horse. A controlled, well-mannered young horse always will be a lot easier to sell, and for more money, than a scared rabbit that's trying to dash for the hills.

Almost any yearling that is fat and sleek is a beautiful animal. Certainly, it has a better appearance than a gaunt, rough-coated one right out of the field, even though a trainer might prefer the latter. The practice of fattening 'em up for the sales, I suppose, is all right. The genuine horseman is able to look through the blubber and see the meat and bone. An overfat yearling doesn't fool anyone of experience, and fewer are presented for sale now than was the case not many years back. Breeders, generally, have hit upon a happy medium, and I believe it's a wise move.

Of course, there are other little details—like do you or don't you trim the ears of a yearling. I don't think it is necessary; it makes the yearling look like a saddle horse or show horse. It isn't necessary to trim the outside or the inside of the ears either, nor is it necessary to have the fetlocks trimmed, or to braid the yearlings. To my mind, a yearling is a young athlete, not something dressed up for show. It is true that braiding may make a bad neck look a little better, but I don't think it is needed at all. If your horses are taught to respond to handling readily, if they are properly fed and adequately exercised, and have the right bloom on them, you have no further problems. I have seen many horses oversell their pedigrees by being presented as racehorses and that is what trainers like to see.

In the twenty years from 1951 to 1970, $250,000,000 worth of yearlings were sold in America, and heaven knows the value of the horses of other ages that changed hands. As big as the business is, it is appropriate that the environment should show some indication of its stature. The sales pavilions of old provided shelter from the rain, seats for the buyers and consignors, rest rooms, and that was about it. I always felt that the consignors and the buyers who were spending big money were entitled to something better. Others agreed, and plans were made, which resulted in a new sales arena at Hialeah Race Course. The facility was designed by John Finney and young Gene Mori, son of the proprietor of Hialeah. It was ready for use in 1962, and it was the first new sales arena erected anywhere since Fasig-Tipton built one in the Lexington paddock in 1927. In 1968, it was enlarged and made a "theater in the round." The rostrum, in the center, revolves so that the announcer and auctioneer face everybody in the seats at one time or another. Closed circuit TVs are placed so that they can be seen by all. When Hialeah's sale of two-year-olds is held, action tapes of the young horses on the racetrack appear on every screen. There are louvered windows for ventilation when the temperature is right.

That was the first of five sales pavilions built according to the company's plans or with the cooperation of Fasig-Tipton. The next one was at Timonium, on the Maryland State Fair grounds. Following that, a pavilion was set up on a smaller scale in Canada at the Woodbine racetrack.

All these pavilions are equipped with an electrically lighted board which shows the number of the horse being sold and each bid as it is being made. The selling price stays up until the next horse comes into the ring. The board has proved immensely popular with the buyers, because it is difficult to keep on top of the bidding with the noise and big crowds milling around. We use it wherever practical. Keeneland installed the board in 1970, because, at the Guggenheim sale, there were many foreigners who might not have been able to understand the auctioneers.

In 1968, our new sales pavilion was opened at Saratoga, and the directors of Fasig-Tipton Company were kind enough to name it for me. The Humphrey S. Finney Pavilion is classic in design and thoroughly functional. It embodies the best features of every horse mart constructed before it. A wide balcony (a good place from which to see how the opposition is bidding) overhangs the main seating area and adds materially to the capacity of the house. There is a covered walking ring behind the main building, with a covered passage leading to it. It is just about everything a sales pavilion should be. More than that, its design makes it suitable for meetings and affairs of all kinds. Civic groups in Saratoga Springs are making good use of it. I am very proud that my associates saw fit to give it my name. It's a pretty big thing to have your name on a building.

One of the finest things that ever has happened to mankind is Saratoga. The pleasant summers and the bubbling springs have been appreciated by residents and visitors for more than two centuries. In 1767, Sir William Johnson, Superintendent of Indian Affairs for Britain, became the first white man to enjoy the healing waters. The baronet bathed in the water and drank of it, and his health improved miraculously. Later pioneers learned to mix it with Scotch, and made the springs a summer resort.

John Morrissey, who had a couple of refined gambling halls going for him in New York City, set up one at the spa. In 1863, Morrissey built a racetrack. Leonard W. Jerome, John R. Hunter and William R. Travers, supplied twenty-six horses for the first meeting, a four-day session, with two races a day. Richard Albert Canfield came along in the '90s. Then came Lily Langtry, James Buchanan Brady (Diamond Jim), Lillian Russell and Victor Herbert.

I didn't get there until 1925. The Grand Union and United States hotels and other big hostelries still were there, as were the gambling houses. I slept on a cot in Sunny Jim Fitzsimmons' tack room and didn't do any gambling to speak of. I was at Saratoga with thirty-five yearlings that Laurel Park Stud had consigned to the sales. Only ten were sold, because of the inordinately high reserves put on the horses. The rest were loaded into vans and hauled back to Maryland, and the heat. But I had gotten a taste of Saratoga's exhilarating weather and pleasant atmosphere and terrain. A few years later, I went back to buy a few yearlings for Sylvester Labrot's Holly Beach Farm. That trip was the clincher. Saratoga was down on the itinerary as a regular stop each summer. I haven't missed many times.

Mornings at Saratoga are the best that nature has to offer. If there is anything better than having melon, scrambled eggs and coffee on the clubhouse porch while watching horses work, I haven't found it. At Saratoga, the people of racing seem relaxed—even the fans. Sure, they are looking for their winners, but they seem to be having a grand time doing it. Saratoga is something special. I hope it remains forever a part of the great Thoroughbred sport. I think it will, because it means so much to so many people.

TWELVE

Time
Marches On

One of the "sick" comedians of our time has said that "Death is Nature's way of warning us to slow down." But then again, Nature does often warn us *before* sending the old gent with the scythe. In the early '50s, I was doing a lot of things and sometimes I must have taken more out of myself than I realized. On September 26, 1954, I got the warning at Garden State Park, during the preview of the New Jersey Yearling Sale. We had no public address system and the wind was blowing very hard, but not much harder than I was, trying to project my voice over the noise of the elements. Suddenly, I didn't have any breath, and I realized that something very bad was happening to me. The next thing I knew, I was in an ambulance, being vanned to Our Lady of Lourdes Hospital, and having oxygen administered to me.

During the time I was on the elevator and being bedded down in the hospital, I was without oxygen, gasping and in a sweating lather. While attendants and nurses were messing around getting the oxygen tent fixed up, I was fighting for breath and thinking about different things, like, "I guess I'll have to get John to come in and handle the sale."

I was sort of between two worlds, but I remember that Dr. Thomas Kain, Jr., vaulted right up onto the bed and jammed both fists and his thumbnails down into my jugular and cut off the flow of blood. Then he released the pressure, and uttered a remark that I'll never forget. "Once in 200 times," he said, "that'll do it."

Dr. Kain had seen that I was in bad shape and had taken emergency measures. As I understand it, what he did was cut off the flow of blood, which eased the pressure on the heart long enough to terminate the spasm. So you'd have to say that his actions saved my life. Of course, I didn't get back to the sale.

My son, John, a sophomore at Princeton at the time, was identifying yearlings on the grounds when I was knocked out of the box. He stepped in to finish the announcing chores and then got permission to leave the university and to run the sale itself. I was pretty sick, but I was proud of the way that youngster stepped in and took over. That was the beginning of a career for John.

I was still grounded by doctor's orders when the Pomona, California sale came up in January 1955. John went West to do the announcing and run the sale. He was no green hand. Though he was not yet twenty-one, he had had experience at Garden State and Belmont and in Maryland; but, as Oscar Otis put it in the *Morning Telegraph*, this marked "his first excursion into the big time pretty much on his own."

I was gratified by the press notices, and I read them with the fervor and satisfaction of a stage mother whose child had been treated well by the critics. Otis said:

"Californians got their first look at announcer John Finney. After the sale, the young man was deluged with congratulations for a job well done. We have reported that young Finney is desirous of carving out a turf career upon the completion of his upcoming three-year tour of duty with the Navy. If his grasp of horses and people, as shown at the sales, is a criterion, his future is quite promising."

In June 1955, John again picked up my burden—and delighted in it. That one, too, was in California—the W. W. Naylor dispersal sale. Naylor, an immense man known to all as "Tiny"—never anything else —had about five very good restaurants around Los Angeles and a ranch down at Riverside. On the day before the sale, Naylor held an all-day preview, showing the stock at his ranch. This is a tactic I like to see used, because it gives buyers a chance to view everything out in the open. Often they are attracted to horses they hadn't even been considering. Late in the afternoon, Tiny served a chuck-wagon dinner on the lawn. About 350 people were on hand to look at the horses and consume the steaks.

The sale was a dandy. Kent Cochran said, in the *Telegraph*, that the "Naylor dispersal of breeding stock here turned out to be the greatest in California since Louis B. Mayer sold his broodmares in 1948."

I was pleased with the sale but was even more pleased with the way John conducted himself, and the reports I received of his poise and promise. I felt a great sense of relief, realizing he was capable of taking a great load off my shoulders. I had put so much of myself into Fasig-Tipton, it was gratifying to see John waiting to be a part of the company and showing tremendous aptitude. He told Bion Abbott of the Los Angeles *Times* that he had felt drawn toward the business of horse-selling since he was about twelve years old. "My first job," he recalled, "was putting hip numbers on horses. At fourteen, I started announcing at shows to get used to the mike. At seventeen, I announced my first horse sale, and the first horse I sold went for $150. In another twenty years, I hope to be able to judge a horse like Pop."

I treasure the clippings, particularly the paragraph that said: "John has a fine voice and a pleasing personality, but he'll never succeed his popular father until he learns how to manipulate his spectacles from the end of his nose." At least, he was leaving me something.

After graduating from Princeton in 1956, *magna cum laude* in English, John served three years in the Navy, becoming a lieutenant (junior grade), and gunnery officer aboard the U.S.S. *Cassin Young*. He enjoyed the Navy and benefited greatly by the experience. After he finished his tour of duty, he came with me at Fasig-Tipton, as an assistant. I was then president and general manager.

In 1959 John married Louise Groves of Newport. For a while they had a tiny apartment in New York City, handy to the Fasig-Tipton office, and then they moved to Connecticut. John and Louise have a girl and a boy, Catherine and Michael.

Olive and I would up with an even division of grandchildren, four colts and four fillies. Pat, our older daughter, has three boys, Douglas, Allan and William, and Marge has three daughters, Macey, Laura and Sarah, all redheads, like their mother. Shortly after she graduated from Missouri's Stephens College in 1950, Pat married V.M.I. graduate Marcus Hansen.

Marge graduated from Randolph-Macon, in 1953, with a Phi Beta Kappa key to treasure. She worked with us at Fasig-Tipton, and married Milton J. (Laddie) Dance, Jr., the company's second auctioneer at that time. They were divorced some years ago, and Marge is now living in Baltimore County. She has been helping Editor Snowden Carter of *The Maryland Horse,* and I must say I'm happy to see the Finney name on the masthead again.

John worked as my assistant at Fasig-Tipton for 18 months. Then in October of 1960 Captain Harry Guggenheim asked me to take over management of his breeding stock in America. To do this I relinquished my position as general manager of Fasig-Tipton, but remained as president. The sales company announced that John had been appointed general manager and that I would remain available for consultation. It was also announced that I would continue my yearly trips to England, still would advise buyers, inspect and purchase horses, and handle insurance and shipping for American clients.

Captain Guggenheim bought his first racehorse in 1934 and remained in racing until his death in 1970 at the age of eighty. "Captain" was no phony title. Guggenheim was a flyer in World War I and flew combat missions in World War II. As a result, all his life he was passionately interested in aerospace development. His family had acquired immense wealth through mining, processing ore, and other activities, but did not sit on the money. Millions were put into institutions and foundations that were to benefit all people. Following the family pattern, Captain Guggenheim left his ninety-acre Falaise Estate to Nassau County, New York, to be used as a recreation and cultural area.

When he was a boy, Guggenheim saw the horses run at Sheepshead Bay, but he really became enamored of the sport while he was at school in Cambridge, and was able to make trips to Newmarket and Paris.

He was one of the most meticulous of men. When he had acquired his Cain Hoy stable, he always insisted that everything be kept in first-class shape. For example, he ordered his trainers never to work a horse in mud, though sometimes they did. Also, he would never have a horse castrated, because he wouldn't have wanted somebody to do that to him.

Immediately after giving up the day-to-day management of Fasig-Tipton, I took over supervision of the Cain Hoy breeding stock. It was Captain Guggenheim's desire to expand his breeding operation to have about fifty broodmares, a large racing stable and a band of two-year-olds coming on each racing season. In the process of expanding, the horses were moved from Claiborne Farm, where they had been for many years, to Leslie Combs' Spendthrift Farm.

Planning breedings, I worked in close cooperation with Combs and with Captain Guggenheim himself. The Captain liked to be right in the middle of things. He spent many an hour over pedigrees, and I would arrange for the breeding of his mares according to an outline that he provided me.

His basic plan was to start every year by breeding his best fifteen mares to his top sire. Actually, I felt that this was a dangerous procedure, since no matter how hard I tried to juggle the horses, we'd end up doing a lot of involuntary inbreeding, and that can lead to a lot of unsoundness. Finally we did open things up a little.

When the young horses became yearlings, I was through with them. They were sent to Falaise, the Guggenheim place at Port Washington, Long Island. There, the trainers took over. I had nothing to do with the racing stable, except when fillies were to be brought to the farm and put into production, or when Captain Guggenheim wanted to sell a draft of racehorses. He dealt directly with his trainers, as far as his racing operation was concerned. And his trainers loved him.

Handling Cain Hoy affairs had made necessary many trips to Kentucky. At least once a month, I spent anywhere from a day to a week in the Blue Grass area. Sometimes, I would be there for as long as two weeks. In 1962, I made seventeen trips from New York to Kentucky and spent seventy-five days in the Campbell House at Lexington. Finally I decided to move my place of residence to Versailles, Kentucky. The rigors of traveling hadn't been doing me any good, and Olive agreed that living in Kentucky would make my work easier.

Between 1938 and 1969, the blue and white blocks of Captain Harry F. Guggenheim's Cain Hoy Stable were carried to victory in thirty-seven stakes races and over 1,000 races in all. Purses earned were in excess of $8,000,000. The stable was the leading money-winner of the nation in 1959 with $742,081, and Cain Hoy's Dark Star, in winning the 1953 Kentucky Derby, was the only horse ever to finish ahead of Alfred Vanderbilt's great Native Dancer.

Through the years, Cain Hoy has bred or been represented by the champions Never Bend and Bald Eagle and the distinguished performers Turn-to, Make Sail, Red Eye, Cherokee Rose, Captain's Gig, Ack Ack, Too Bald, One-Eyed King, Never Bow, Battle Joined, Ragusa and Red God. After World War II, Captain Guggenheim collected as much as he could of the best blood of Nearco, and the influence of his planned breeding has been felt in America and abroad.

Turn-to, bought as a yearling, sired First Landing, leading two-year-old of '58; Hail to Reason, which won the same honor in '60; Cyane, Futurity and Dwyer winner; Captain's Gig, Futurity winner; Sir Gaylord, and a score of other stakes winners. Hail to Reason has sired Proud Clarion, a Kentucky Derby winner; Hail to All, a Belmont Stakes winner; Straight Deal, considered the best handicap mare of 1967; Woozem, Admiring, Priceless Gem; Personality and a long string of others. Red Eye, a filly by Petee-Wrack, won the Ladies and Gazelle Handicaps in 1939 for Cain Hoy, and produced Fantan, dam of the great racehorse, Ragusa, a top in his generation in England. Siama, which won the Acorn, Jasmine, Monmouth Oaks and Princess Doreen Stakes, and Comely Handicap, later became the mother of Bald Eagle, One-Eyed King and Dead Ahead. Never Bend (Nasrullah—Lalun, by Djeddah), bred by Cain Hoy, was rated first in the Experimental Handicap of 1962 at 126 pounds. He won the Futurity, Champagne and Cowdin at two, and the Flamingo Stakes and Yankee Handicap at three. He was second in the Kentucky Derby (to Chateaugay); in the Woodward (to Kelso); and in the United Nations (to Mongo). In two seasons, he earned $641,524—$402,969 as a two-year-old, then a record.

In February 1964, Never Bend was sold to Leslie Combs II, who syndicated him at $40,000 a share. I hated to see him sold, though Cain Hoy bought back five shares. I felt that Never Bend was the best prospect the stable ever had. He was a top miler with great speed, the pattern of most successful sires. I guess I wasn't far wrong as his first four crops had earned $2,129,625 through 1970. Never Bend was quick to achieve a distinction which eludes many top horses—that of siring a horse as good as he was. His Mill Reef won the Epsom Derby and Prix de l'Arc de Triomphe and was European champion as a three-year-old in 1971. After a near fatal training accident the following season, he recovered and was syndicated for stud in 1973 for $5,000,000.

The story goes on and on, and it is a wonderful demonstration of what the results of selective breeding can be. It also confirms Captain Guggenheim's acumen in the field of Thoroughbred production. Working for and with such a man was indeed a pleasure and privilege, and I believe it furthered my education. There is always something more to learn in this great game.

On September 29, 1969, Captain Guggenheim announced his retirement and his decision to make a complete dispersal at auction of the stable's Thoroughbred racing and breeding stock. That statement meant that my office as manager of the Cain Hoy American breeding interests was no more; but it also launched another sale of Thoroughbreds staggering in immensity. The broodmares—fifty-one of them—and twenty-nine weanlings were offered at Keeneland on November 14, and thirty yearlings and twenty-seven racehorses went through the ring at Belmont Park on November 17. When the money was counted, the figures showed that $4,751,200 had been paid for the 137 Thoroughbreds—an average of $34,680!

With the quality of stock offered, nobody expected to "steal" anything. The people who came to bid were there to buy top-quality horses, and predictions were that the battles were to be in big numbers. Auctioneers always are optimistic, and often ask for an opening offer flattering to the animal in the ring. In this sale, suave George Swinebroad was suggesting opening bids of $20,000—and getting them! The weanlings averaged $26,007 (and only a few years before the record for a horse less than one year old was $22,000). A new world record for a weanling was set when trainer Arnold Winick paid $110,000 for a filly by Turn-to—Polly Girl, by Prince Bio. Winick was acting for bookmaking magnate William Hill, of London. Polly Girl, offered just before her daughter, was bought by Mrs. Ogden Phipps for $160,000, with A. B. Hancock, Jr., doing the bidding.

Six of the eighty horses offered at Keeneland went for $100,000 or more. The stakes mare, Too Bald, brought top price—$225,000. Bidding on the five-year-old daughter of Bald Eagle—Hidden Talent, by Dark Star, started at $50,000. Charles W. Engelhard bought her for his Cragwood Stable.

When the shelves were cleared in Kentucky, the buyers hastened to New York, where the game continued at big stakes. Robert J. Kleberg paid $175,000 for Ribot's Fan, a two-year-old filly, and gave $100,000 for a yearling colt by Ambiorix, out of Make Sail. Rokeby Stable took a Graustark yearling filly for $110,000, and John M. Olin went to $100,000 for a yearling colt by Never Bend. The twenty-seven horses of racing age averaged $30,408, and the thirty yearlings, $31,933.

Upon the death of Captain Guggenheim, the estate sold Ack Ack to E. E. (Buddy) Fogelson and his wife, Greer Garson. Six days before the Captain had died, Ack Ack had won the San Carlos. For the Fogelsons, he added a number of top stakes, and finished the season as Horse of the Year 1971. The Captain would have been very proud.

THIRTEEN

Around the World

For the man who is forced to pursue an occupation that is distasteful to him, I have a feeling of great pity. In the turf world, I can't recall ever having met anyone who didn't like what he was doing. He might not like the person for whom he was doing it, but the work itself was his "thing," as some of our young folk put it. Whether it is tidying up the bed-chamber of a horse on the backstretch, or cheering for a homebred Derby winner, or watching a yearling sell for a better-than-predicted price, horsefolk always seem to be intensely interested in what they're doing. Few would swap places with anyone else, though they might be delighted to swap some of their horses.

All through life I have felt a compulsion to see as much as possible of the world's Thoroughbred production areas and racing centers, and to learn what I could of methods and practices in other countries. And I have always made a point of talking to other horsemen wherever I went. Long ago, I discovered that listening to great horsemen is a means to a better education in the field. I never have stopped learning, and I treasure the bull sessions I have had with people attached to racing and Thoroughbred breeding.

From 1948 to 1970 I made thirteen trips to Europe. Excluding 1954, when I had my heart attack, I attended the Newmarket Sales every year from '50 to '59. In 1956 I was overseas twice. I went again to Newmarket in '67 and then again in '69. Usually, when going to Europe, I had commitments to buy horses for American breeders or people with racing stables. Always, I enjoyed these visits, broadening my acquaintanceship among the horsefolk, and meeting old friends from all over the world at Newmarket.

Anyone accustomed to horse sales in America would marvel at the way the famous December Sales at Newmarket are held by Tattersalls, the great English sales company. The sales start in the morning, about nine o'clock, and horses are auctioned continuously—no recesses—until about eight at night, maybe later. About five auctioneers work. Each will sell ten or fifteen horses and then give way to another, rotating in sequence. Always, there is one in the stand and four in reserve. If a consignor wishes to have his horses sold by a certain auctioneer, the schedule of turns is broken temporarily, and picked up after that lot goes through the ring. In the restaurant, hard by the sales ring, there is a table reserved for Tattersalls. In relays the people associated with the sales company have lunch and, later, tea. They always are on the grounds.

The way the order of selling is arranged for the week of the December Sales is very interesting. If there is a dispersal of the stock of a deceased owner, it is put on first thing in the morning. Dead men's horses go first. I suppose the idea is that there won't be any complaints from consignors although there might be some protests from the heirs. If the consignment is a large one, it may be divided into two or three groups, and sold on Tuesday, Wednesday and Thursday mornings, the best days of the sale. That was done with Robert Sterling Clark's horses.

When there is no dispersal, the sale will begin with horses that are considered something less than the stars of the program. The quality and the prices will build up as the morning progresses, and the high point will be reached around noon. From about 12:30 to 2:30, quality, interest and prices will sag. Invariably, less than top-class animals will be offered. Then, another peak will be reached at about 4:30, followed by another dip (teatime), then a rise to a final crescendo.

When horses of all ages are sold, mares and foals go first—in the morning—and horses in training are sold in the late afternoon and evening. Working up the catalogue must be a very complex task.

The horses are stabled all over the countryside within about ten miles of the sales center. There may be 700 or 800 horses stabled in close proximity to the arena, and more move in as these move out.

Before the sale, the horses are walked around a large ring, maybe 200 yards in diameter. Then they move into a smaller circle, and finally into the sales ring. The presentation of racehorses in the sales arena is a remarkable sight. The horses are ridden into the ring. They are blanketed, and many are wearing hoods and boots or bandages. The neck hoods cover them to the saddle, the quarter blanket, to the quarters. There's very little to see of a horse while he is being put up for sale. Anyone interested in a particular horse had better get there ahead of time and find it in its stall if he wants to have a look at it.

The sales ring is larger than those in America—about forty feet across. People sit all around the ring and can see the horses move much better than they can in our sales rings. During the week, as many as 1,600 horses may be sold.

On one of our visits with Noel Murless, one of England's leading trainers, and his wife Gwen, we were guests at evening "stables" and dinner. "Stables" is something of a ritual. At about 5:45, the trainer and his guests make a tour of inspection of all the horses in the yard. A stable lad provides a bunch of grass or a carrot to keep the horse happy, and will have his charge brushed to a "T". When the trainer enters the stall, the lad will stand the horse up for inspection. The trainer may tell the boy to "turn him around," may feel the horse's legs, or pick up his feet, often making comments to his guests. The guests make diplomatic comments, if any. Sometimes, visitors are asked for tea and stables, and sometimes for stables and dinner, depending upon the popularity of the guests with the trainer, or the desirability of having them around.

My heart attack and other ailments did not prevent Olive and me from attending the 1958 Newmarket Sales, and I enjoyed my first Gimcrack Dinner as the guest of Marcus Wickham-Boynton, breeder of many winners at Burton Agnes Stud. The Gimcrack Stakes is a summer feature for two-year-olds, at York, and the owner of the winner is the honored guest at the Dinner in December. He is toasted and given the opportunity to speak on any facet of racing. He may air a gripe, or recommend changes that he thinks will improve the sport (or make things better for him, personally).

The six-furlong race was inaugurated in 1846, and the Dinner has become an institution of English racing. It is put on each year by "the Ancient Fraternitie of York Gimcracks," an association made up of about eighty prominent turf personalities—members of The Jockey Club, owners, trainers and jockeys. It is an extremely colorful affair. Hunting attire is worn by hunt club members and those attached to the armed forces appear in military full dress. The majority of guests wear black tie, but quite a number go all the way with white tie and tails. The "for men only" sign was hung out at the Gimcrack Dinner from the time it was inaugurated until the race was won by Mrs. Parker Poe's Young Emperor in 1965. Mrs. Poe attended the dinner, but didn't make the speech. Mr. Poe read it for her.

Lord Irwin, Earl of Halifax, was president of the Gimcrack Club and ran the show. William Hill, the bookmaker, had won the Gimcrack Stakes that year with Be Careful (which seems to be an appropriate name for a bookie's horse), so he was toasted and was permitted to "sound off." He wrenched the heartstrings of his listeners when he spoke on the "precarious living" of the bookmaker. He suggested changes in the method of handling and controlling betting so that bookmakers might enjoy reasonable security. Be Careful, incidentally, was bred by Phil Bull, publisher of *Timeform,* which is the most valuable tool the English have for intelligent handicapping. It is an invaluable summation of the class of all horses racing in the United Kingdom and Eire.

Since many of those attending Gimcrack Dinners are members of hunt clubs, a fox hunt is appropriate as a finale. This event is held the morning after the Dinner. Headache or no, all dinner guests are welcome to participate. Lord Irwin was master of his own pack of hounds, and the morning after the Dinner I attended, he sent them out to find a fox. I didn't wait to learn if they found one. I was off on my favorite pursuit—visiting horse farms.

When visiting other lands, it is natural to compare the methods used with those employed in the United States. In my travels through England, Ireland and France I was impressed most of all by the independence of the trainer. The owner, of course, has the final say, and may have some ideas of his own about the program for a particular horse, but in most cases, complete reliance is placed on the trainer. There is little meddling. With some trainers, an owner wouldn't dare to dictate. One trainer I know became absolutely furious when his patron insisted upon altering a horse's racing schedule.

A trainer is engaged because he is skilled in his profession. His perpetuation in office depends upon his ability to get the best out of the horses under his management. He stands and falls on what he does; and he has a better chance of standing if his activities are not inhibited in any way. I know many English, Irish and French trainers personally. They are serious, proud men, confident in the methods they have tested through experience.

Europe isn't the only place that my fascination with horses has led me. I've also traveled several times to the south and east—from Peru, Chile, and Argentina to Australia and New Zealand to Japan, with plenty of stops in between.

One of the highlights of all these travels was my visits in 1963 and 1968 to Frank Thompson's famous Widden Stud near Sydney, Australia. I had been promising myself that I would visit there someday ever since 1952, when Frank Thompson and I had been sitting out London's worst-ever fog, and along with helping me observe the elbow-bending rites that go along with waiting out fogs, Frank had been telling me about the wonders of his country, with special emphasis on the Thoroughbred and the people and places associated therewith. Frank vowed that, should time and circumstances allow me to visit the Island Continent, he would act as reception committee and guide, and guarantee an interesting visit.

Frank's invitation was filed for future action. Then, early in 1963, I took it out of the file and made my first trip to Australia.

On January 29th, we arrived in Sydney, and Frank Thompson, just as he had promised eleven years earlier, was at the airport to greet us. He stayed with us throughout a tour of three of the six political subdivisions that make up the Australian mainland, taking us to places we never would have seen without his guidance.

Thompson's Widden Stud housed the Thoroughbred portion of King Ranch's Australian division—the last youngsters by Bob Kleberg's Flying Missel were at Widden in 1963. At times, there isn't much water in Widden Creek, but this wasn't one of those times. As a result of prolonged and heavy summer rains, the stream was at flood stage. Roads were under water and travel by motor car was impracticable, to say the least. The plane had put us down on Widden airstrip, so we stayed put and had a fine time looking at horses and checking pedigrees of the mares. When it was possible to cross the creek in a wagon pulled by a high-wheel tractor, we went off to see more stud farms.

All the stud farms in the area raised some cattle, but no sheep. At Widden Stud, Frank Thompson had built up the finest herd of Santa Gertrudis cattle outside of the United States. The farm for many years had raised shorthorns, but Santa Gertrudis bulls had about bred out the shorthorn blood in the grade herd. Many winners of the carcass class at the Sydney Royal show have come from that herd. Widden Stud is managed by Thompson's son James W., better known to the horse world as "Bim." This young man had a period of study at Spendthrift and other Kentucky farms, and spent some time with members of the famous veterinary firm of Hagyard, Davidson and McGee.

In 1968, the next time I was in Sydney, I had another great opportunity—Thomas John Smith, long-time leading trainer in Australia, invited me to visit him to observe his training procedures. Smith's lifetime record is lost in limbo, as there was no statistical service, but, in each of the five years previous to the 1967–68 season, he had trained over 100 winners, with 117 his most recent mark. The season in Australia starts August 1, and at the time of my visit, Smith had met sixty-eight horses in the winner's circle, with five months still to go in the racing year.

A smallish, quiet man, Tom was born in Griffiths, New South Wales in 1917. His father was a butcher and raced a few horses at the "country" meetings. Tommy, as a boy, rode broncos and was a champion show-ring rider. He was apprenticed to Matt Sawyer, and rode on the flat and over hurdles. A fall terminated his saddle career. He still has the slightly bowed, rolling gait of the cowboy.

Though his looks belie it, Smith is a dynamo of energy. At 5:15 a.m., one hot, sticky morning, he picked me up at the Australia Hotel, and off we went to Tulloch Lodge, near Randwick Race Course, where his stable and office are situated. "This place was paid for by Tulloch," said Tommy. He had bought the bay horse for a song at the New Zealand sales and later passed him on to A. E. Haley but continued to train him. Tulloch won thirty-six races and was sixteen other times in the money, earning 110,123½ pounds, for an Australian record.

"Randwick," Smith said, "is the finest training course I have found in the world. It can take one of Sydney's ten-inch rainfalls and still offer good galloping the next day." Inside Randwick's main 1⅜-mile oval were five grass courses, one tanbark strip and one sand track.

Dawn was breaking when we reached Tulloch Lodge. We were met by Tom's brother, Ernie, who served as stable foreman, head lad and assistant trainer. The brothers sat at opposite sides of a desk and discussed the program for the morning—how the horses were to be paired off for work, who would ride which, and the condition of each horse. Another brother, Dick, proprietor of a sporting pub (as hotels are called in New South Wales) and breeder and owner of a few racehorses, joined us for the training period. Ernie and Dick, tall and lean, and Tom, short and stocky, made a great trio, and there never was a dull moment throughout the training session. The kidding going on among the three provided lively background for the serious business of training horses.

From Tulloch Lodge we drove to the racecourse, where we left the car and walked across Randwick's several courses to an elevated trailer in the infield. The vehicle was about twelve feet long and eight wide, with wheels on one end and chocks under the other. The floor was about four and a half feet off the ground. Louvered glass windows gave protection, and wide visibility. From that point of vantage, the trainers watched the workouts. "The Little General," Dick's term for Tom, shouted orders as the horses came up in singles, pairs or trios after being trotted across the track from the "holding stalls" (saddling paddocks). The forty-eight horses in training had been out for forty-five minutes of walking, under Ernie's supervision, before we got there.

About twenty-five exercise boys took the horses out to the training area. Most of the boys were ponying one or two other horses in addition to handling their own mounts. Entire (uncastrated) colts received no special attention. A boy might be riding a colt and leading a filly on one side and a gelding on the other. And there was no monkey business.

The stable jockey, Australian George Moore, had had phenomenal success with Noel Murless in England in 1967. I watched him work seven horses that morning, and his horsemanship was a joy to behold. He had to be one of the outstanding riders of his time.

The horses were trotted about until called in for work orders. Riders then were changed and Smith shouted instructions while standing in the doorway of the trailer. Several sets of his horses worked at different distances at the same time. In each hand, Smith held a watch almost as big as an alarm clock. "Clarence the Clocker," his assistant, was similarly armed, and the two men were able to clock several horses simultaneously. Clarence proved his dexterity of mind and hand by recording the times on a sheet that listed singles, trios and pairs to be worked, and the rider of each horse.

In all the years I have observed training procedures throughout the world, I never have seen anything like Smith's operation. We went onto the trailer-stand at 5:50 a.m., and left it at 6:50 a.m.—after forty-eight horses had been worked. During that hour, Smith moved from side to side in the stand, jumped down now and then for a word with a rider, waved the slow-goers to the outside, called times to Clarence, compared figures with those of other work watchers and had an eye on everything that was going on. The thought came to my mind that this man must have at least double vision. With so many horses, different distances of the works and varied paces, it was impossible for a casual observer to know what the hell was going on.

Smith's horses were lean and looked hard as nails. He kept his in-training horses galloping daily—even on the day after a race. They were well muscled-up, and appeared fit for anything—and they had to be. In an eight-day meeting, such as a "Spring Carnival," it was not unusual for a high-class horse to get into three races.

The horses wore flat steel shoes weighing about six ounces while working, but would be reshod with aluminum plates when sent to racing. No heel calks or toes of any kind were allowed. The workouts that I saw ranged in extent from three to nine furlongs, depending

upon the distance of the horse's next race. After the run, they were
hosed off in the holding stalls, and then walked through the streets
back to their stables. At home, they were given five minutes of inhala-
tion through a nosebag, connected to an oxygen tank. (Smith's horses
were also given oxygen before going out to race.) Then each horse was
turned into a sand yard, so he could enjoy a roll.

Smith fed a mixture of whole oats (no crushed oats for him),
cracked corn (maize), crushed peas, some bran and a little cut chaff,
with good hay used for this. Glucose was given when required as was
powdered milk.

An elementary school playground lay beside Smith's stable, and
during recesses and before and after school, there was plenty of noise.
Smith said he thought the din was helpful, because it accustomed
nervous horses to unusual noises and helped settle them down. "Ra-
dios help, too," he said.

Smith had five lead ponies in his stable, and these were busy
animals. Fillies never were ridden, except for fast works, so the ponies
logged many a mile escorting the females through their exercises.
When Smith set himself up in the training profession, many years ago,
he bought seven yearlings at the Sydney Easter Sale. All of them won,
so he must have been born with an eye for a good horse.

In Australia and New Zealand, I found areas that couldn't be
improved upon for horse production. The salubrious climate makes
pasturing possible the year around, and the grass is about as good as
is found anywhere. Even in places affected by drought, the animals
were kept up to par through the use of good hay and supplements.
Nearly everywhere, the foals may be allowed outside immediately after
birth. Most are foaled out-of-doors, and foals are running on excellent
grass from the time they hit the ground. The young horses, for the
most part, were well grown. With few exceptions, the hundreds I saw
were of proper size and development for their age.

A fact that impressed me everywhere in Australia was the prodi-
gious number of mares each stallion was able to get in foal. Breeders
think nothing of booking fifty or sixty mares to a horse. I checked the
records of a number of sires, and came to the conclusion that the ratio
of pregnancies to matings is higher in Australia than in the United

States. The natural conditions under which the horses are reared, and the lack of artificiality in the operation, must have some effect. But I believe that the most important factor is that few mares are shipped away from the home farm for breeding. In the yearling catalogues, the majority of the progeny of any stallion comes from the stud of his owner.

Another interesting point regarding breeding: I noticed that many —perhaps most—of the stallions practicing their trade in Australia were not foaled there. A high percentage came from England. Breeders told me that they absolutely had to import, as few of the native-bred sires could stand up to competition. I suspect that this belief is something of a fetish, but I admit that I have been told that many really top-class homebreds have gone to stud in Australia, and failed to live up to expectations. On the other hand, numerous moderate animals have been imported as sires and have achieved amazing success.

All through Australia and New Zealand there are families who have raised horses for generations, and the attitude toward the business is casual, as it is in the long-established breeding farms in America or Europe.

My impression of Japan was quite different. All preconceived notions go out the window when you visit this aggressively forward-moving country. There were horses and races there before World War II, but the industry has surged ahead during postbellum years. The Japanese now seem to be almost obsessed with the idea of building up and perfecting the horse industry as quickly as possible.

The Japan Racing Association, an active, effective organization, has complete control of top-level Japanese racing, and, indirectly, of breeding. It maintains nine racecourses, operating throughout the islands on Saturdays, Sundays and holidays and has a first-class jockeys' training school at Equestrian Park in Tokyo, where some of the equine events of the Olympic games were held in 1964. The Association also has a complete Equine Health Laboratory, where all sorts of projects are under investigation. Among the projects, besides testing saliva and urine samples from the racecourse, are research on nutrition and metabolism, physical activity and fatigue, cardiography and phonography of heart function, equine health management, bone troubles, influenza and "the cough," and horseshoeing and foot care.

The jockey school is an institution of incalculable value to the sport of racing in Japan. Boys who would be riders are chosen for aptitude and size. A candidate must have graduated from junior high school, and is required to pass entrance examinations in the Japanese language, mathematics, and social studies. He must be under twenty years of age, less than sixty-one inches in height and under eighty-eight pounds in weight, and must be "free of color blindness and tuberculosis."

The regular school term is two years. Beginning students spend two months becoming accustomed to handling horses (many have never touched a horse before) and learning to stay in the saddle. Four months of applied training follow. The later portion emphasizes steeplechase riding. Advanced training during the last half of the year includes short-stirrup riding and high-speed race riding.

Two hours in the morning are devoted to riding technique; two in the afternoon to academic instruction. The students are taught hippology, the rules of racing, diet, and gymnastics. Stress is placed upon fair play and good sportsmanship. Each student is responsible for the care of two horses, and learns stable practice from the ground up—literally.

Five one-month courses are also included each year. Short-term students are riders who have been working for trainers and who have qualified as jockey candidates. These lads are under three-year contracts, and must go through at least three short-term sessions before they are permitted to take the license examination. While learning, students are supported by the JRA.

Sitting in the director's room—sipping green tea—I watched a class of ten junior students walk, trot and canter their mounts in various figures in an exercise ring just below the window. First-year boys executed figure eights at all gaits, sitting flat without stirrups. They reversed, moved into pairs and performed other routines designed to teach them how to keep their horses under proper control. They also practiced dismounting, vaulting over the horse's back from either side and remounting without aid. At the far end of the ring was a class of eight seniors who were sending their horses over a course of Olympic-type fences in rapid succession. They had returned from trainers' stables for final polishing before graduation. All were attired in the neat red caps and jerseys of the JRA.

In 1968, there were about 200 jockeys active in national racing in Japan. About 55 per cent of them were graduates of the full course, 38 per cent had received short-term training and the others qualified as jockeys before the training system was instituted.

The postwar renaissance of racing and breeding in Japan has resulted in the best organizational setup in the world today. In the relatively small area involved and the limited number of horses, an autonomy such as the Japan Racing Association functions perfectly. Breeders, owners, track managements, veterinarians and jockeys all operate at top efficiency through coordination and cooperation.

The Association is virtually an arm of the government, and all activities are channeled through the organization. In the United States, every state has its own racing commission and laws, tracks operate independently, and no one agency has authority over all. I guess it would be impossible to set up an institution requiring coordination of all states and tracks in North America, but it's a beautiful dream.

FOURTEEN

On Buying
Horses

Balance and proportion are combined in the make-up of a fine individual. In the mind of every worthy trainer or experienced show judge, there is an ideal horse of the breed he is examining. The word "quality" is frequently used by Thoroughbred folk—he has "quality" or, he is a "quality horse." This means that the animal pleases the eye of the observer and fits into the mold he has mentally established for the breed. Sometimes this quality registers at a glance, sometimes a long look is necessary. It is not unusual to hear a trainer say: "Over all, he doesn't impress me, but when you take him apart, you can't find anything to fault."

In buying Thoroughbred yearlings, sometimes you're right and sometimes you're wrong. Many factors guide you in forming your judgments, but you've got to have confidence in your own ability. Some people have a great eye for horses in the raw—young ones. Max Hirsch could see more in yearlings than anyone I've ever known. Frequently, Max would buy a horse that fell far short of physical perfection, but he saw things that others missed, and ended up with good racehorses. Possibly, Hirsch could recognize in the horse's attitude or actions that indescribable something generally termed "the will to win." That counterbalances many physical defects.

Those not gifted with such delicate perception must judge a horse solely by its physical attributes. So you must have that model of the perfect horse in your mind's eye and come as close to that model as you can. Even then, the perfect physical specimen very often is not the perfect performer—by a long stretch.

Nearly all horses have some defects. Many great horses have had physical deformities or deficiencies which they were able to overcome. It is the same with human beings. The right heart and mentality enable them to rise above physical shortcomings and become great men and women. Tenny, Salvator's arch-rival of the 1890s, was a swayback. The fans called him the Swayback Bay. Assault, with a clubfoot, but an iron heart, won the Triple Crown and many other races for King Ranch. Miss Cavandish was culled out by the same stable and picked up by Harry S. Nichols as a yearling for $1,500. Trained by Roger Laurin, Miss Cavandish became a wonderful racer. Roger handled her with extreme care and patience. Her heart overcame the handicap of her crooked legs and weak underpinning.

An even more classic example was Boojiana, a racemare with terribly deformed ankles. She was by Boojum, an unsound horse himself. He had big puffball ankles, but tremendous speed. When Boojiana was a yearling, you wouldn't have given a nickel for her chances. C. V. Whitney bred her and turned her over to Andy Schuttinger to train. At two, she won the Matron and the Schuylerville and at three, the Top Flight Handicap. When sent to the stud, she produced some unsound horses but they all had ability.

These were some of the exceptions that found greatness, because they had it in them, and because they were in the hands of master horsemen who were able to bring it out. In the long run, though, you will do far better by passing over the ones with obvious imperfections. If you're a buyer, you get the best you can for the money you have. If you're a breeder, you take what the good Lord gives you and hope for the best.

In the final analysis what you have to do first is to look over the whole animal, then eliminate the faults and see how much is good after you have seen the defects. Then you have to balance the defects against the overall good. It's the overall balance you are figuring on.

Carroll Reid, who trained for the Labrots and managed Holly Beach for a period, often said that in picking out a mare he looked for one with "a good countenance." He meant that the head, the eye and the ear had to be right before he would look further. Like everything else you can say about horses, there are exceptions to this rule of his, but a horse that seems alert and aware of what's going on around him is more likely to draw you to him than one that appears dopey.

Some horses seem sluggish as hell and you wouldn't give a nickel for them if you saw them walking around. They plod to the post like cows, then suddenly come alive under the pressure of racing and reveal their real talents. These, however, are the exceptions. Generally, it's the intelligent-looking animals—and you can see when they are intelligent—that are most likely to develop into something.

They used to say in England, "You want a good, big, full eye—one that you can knock off with a stick." That's about it. Janon Fisher, Jr., who trained Blockade to win the Maryland Hunt Cup three times and Mountain Dew to take the same difficult event the same number of times, attributed Blockade's ability, in part at least, to his wonderful eyes. With his remarkable vision, he could see his fences well and measure them accurately. Photos of Blockade show great, big eyes that stand out. I would steer away from a pig-eyed horse, one with a small eye that gives him a mean look. There should be plenty of breadth between the eyes. There are a number of things to look for when you're sizing up a horse. A good, flat forehead is preferable. A slightly dished (concave) face may be all right, but you don't go around looking for that kind. If nothing else, it just looks weak. The head should be well set on and join with the neck as though it belongs there. A head awkwardly pitched—drawn up like a rooster's—can affect the breathing. I would consider as a fault a "keg" head—a rough, barrel-type skull that shows coarseness.

A Roman nose is not a real defect in a horse. Generally, Roman-nosed horses are pretty determined, either the right way or the wrong way. When you've taught one to jump, you've got a good jumper, though sometimes it takes a lot of teaching. And they don't look as handsome in the show ring as an animal with classic physiognomy.

I like a well-set-on pair of ears that go up to indicate alertness and interest in what's going on. Lop ears occur occasionally, and, while they give a horse a droopy look, it doesn't follow that he should be listless of character. There have been very good racehorses with lop ears. Like the Roman nose, though, they wouldn't help in show conformation classes.

The jaw should be deep and wide with the muscle showing—a strong jaw. There should be room enough to shove your clenched fist up between the jaw bones. That gives plenty of room for the breathing apparatus. A fine throat should be ample, but not coarse, and the neck should be heavier in the male than in the female, and be in proportion to the head. A big head and a scrawny neck or a little light head on a thick neck, throws the whole system of anatomy out of balance.

A well-developed wither is desirable, and it should go smoothly into a nice oblique shoulder. Too sharp a wither is not good. The back should be strong and not dip sharply, nor should it bulge upward— roachbacked is what they call it. The quarters should be well rounded, with the hind leg coming straight down. You should be able to drop a perpendicular from the point of the buttocks right down the back of the hind tendon. In a sprinter, the quarters usually are well developed as is the muscling in the forearm, the thigh and the second thigh. The staying type of horse usually is long and lean and doesn't carry any excess weight. The sprinter uses his great strength to accelerate rapidly. The router starts more casually and swings along at an easier pace.

The tail is a part of a horse that can indicate quality. I don't mean a long, flowing, beautiful ornament. I mean the bone and muscle in the tail. I like to run my hand down a horse's back and pick up his tail and see how much strength is there. I hate a horse with a tail that you can flip here, there and everywhere with a finger. If a horse has a fine, strong tail bone, he's likely to be well-boned and tough-sinewed throughout. A big, meaty tail bone and a loose tail can indicate poor bone structure, as well as general softness. Of course, when you look at a mare, you lift her tail to see that the vulva is perpendicular. If the upper part slopes forward, droppings can be drawn in. That invites infection.

The shoulder should have about a 45-degree angle slope to give a horse freedom to stretch out when in action. In a running horse, a nice sloping shoulder brings joy to a trainer's heart. Some make that the starting point when examining a horse. A straight shoulder inhibits the horse's action. I never saw a top-class racehorse that didn't have a good shoulder.

No matter what the breed, a horse's leg should swing straight forward to give the best action and the most efficient use of the running and driving gear. All four legs should point directly ahead, and should appear straight when viewed fore and aft. Straight action means free action—smooth action. The bone in the leg should be rock-hard and straight. It should not "cut in" below the knee, though there have been some great horses that were "over at the knee"—Bahram, Discovery, and St. Simon among them. Few horses that amount to much are back at the knee—"calf-kneed"—though there are notable exceptions here too. Never Say Die was slightly calf-kneed.

The line of the front leg should go down the forearm to the knee and continue through the knee and into the cannon bone without any sharp break. That's the side view, of course. From the front, the leg should be straight. It shouldn't bow out, and it certainly shouldn't be knock-kneed.

Look for a straight line from the side and from the front. From the rear, the hind legs should be straight. A horse with legs that go here, there and everywhere is always likely to injure himself, aside from being less efficient because of out-of-line legs. Sickle hocks, that appear bent when viewed from the side—or "cow hocks," that tend to point in, toward each other, when viewed from the rear—are considered undesirable. Many stallions which are sickle-hocked get sickle-hocked stock. A lot of them can run, but all would be better off for having a good straight hind leg. That's perfection.

When you look at a horse walking away from you, the legs should be in track, each hind leg following directly behind the foreleg on the same side. Watching from the side, I like to see a horse stride out, as though he enjoys moving.

A normal foot is neither too steep nor too wide and flat. About a 45-degree slope from a good rounded toe and with good wide heels is what you want. A flat foot is often found in horses imported from the European countries where young horses are usually out in lush wet grazing. It takes quite a time to get the average imported animal's feet in good shape for American racing. The foot should hit the ground fair and square, neither side being higher or lower than the other, and the frog should have contact with the ground.

A brittle, shelly foot is a curse often found. And there's no doubt that white feet do have a tendency to be softer than dark ones. A tough black foot is the most desirable. There used to be an old saying which, like a lot of old wives' tales, doesn't go for much nowadays and it ran like this:

> One white foot, ride him for your life,
> Two white feet, give him to your wife,
> Three white feet, send him far away,
> Four white feet, keep him not a day.

There's not too much truth to that though—just look at white legged and footed horses like Secretariat and Your Host and Jolly Roger, Mrs. Whitney's great old jumper that stood up and trained for years very successfully. Horses can run on all kinds of feet if they are properly cared for. But if all other things are equal, take the dark-footed horse over the white-footed horse, because you're more likely to be right.

Always pick up a horse's feet and look at them to see if and how they have been trimmed. This way you can tell whether his hoofs have been trimmed to throw him one way or the other. When his ankle is resting in your hand, the pastern and foot swing on their natural hinge. You can see at once if corrective trimming has been done by observing whether the floor of the hoof is at right angles to the natural suspension of the foot.

Nowadays almost all horses are shod and much attention is paid to shoeing. Shoes give the hoof protection—prevent it from breaking and give the horse a better grip on the running surface. The trainer should settle for nothing short of absolute perfection in the matter of the hoof for all horses in training. Correct shoeing can help many horses to stay sound and active; careless work on the feet can ruin a horse's chances.

The quality of potential greatness in a horse that trainer Max Hirsch was able to recognize is not easy to describe or identify. It is an intangible factor that makes the difference between a good horse and an ordinary one. It is a combination of something that exists in the heart of the animal and his will to win. You look for it in the pedigree and in the animal's expression, but you don't really know that it's there until the horse shows you. Until he does, you don't know whether he's chicken or has a good game heart.

Trainer Carroll Reid believed a valuable clue could be found in the horse's expression, at least where broodmares were concerned. I learned a lot from Reid when I accompanied him to the Fall Sales at Lexington to buy broodmares. At that time, Fasig-Tipton had a parcel of about five or six acres of land on the Paris Pike, with the sales pavilion nearest the road. Four or five rows of Saratoga style barns fanned out behind the pavilion. There were no screens in the doors and many of the mares would stand with their heads out watching what was going on.

From the catalogue I used to pick the ones whose pedigrees I liked, the ones with the most fashionable breeding and the best production records—those that looked best "on paper." I wanted to look at them more closely, but Mr. Reid said, "No. Just wait awhile." So we stood there and watched the mares. Well, some of the mares looked interested in the activities about them, some of them just stared off into space and others let their heads hang droopily. I said, "Let's go and see No. 28."

"No, don't want to see it," Mr. Reid responded.

"Why not?" I argued. "It's by So-and-so and has produced Such-a-one."

"Ain't got a good countenance," the trainer told me.

"What do you mean, Mr. Reid?" I asked.

"I never saw a good broodmare that didn't have a motherly look," he concluded.

And that's about ninety per cent right. Rarely do you find a good animal that does not typify its sex. Mothers of families look like mothers of families. Your Amazon types—as a rule—are just not good producers (although their daughters often are).

After sizing up her countenance, you look over the mare herself. She should be an attractive, straight-legged animal with a good feminine look, deep through the heart, and a nice free mover, without discernible blemish, if possible. There are few perfect individuals to be found, so one must evaluate any deviation from the norm to see how important it might be. To me a calf-knee is about the worst defect a mare might have. I also hate to look at a splay-footed mare. Bent hocks can be tolerated and rate about like a pigeon-toe, but a good straight hind leg is most desirable.

Broodmares should be kept in nice flesh, not overfat by all means, and not too thin either, though most veteran horsemen feel a thin, thrifty mare in good health will conceive easier than a fat one. Mares need their feet trimmed regularly, or if they require shoeing, the shoes should be looked at at least once a month. The nearer to nature mares are kept, the better it is for them. They can run out day and night, with a shed for shelter, but they need to be brought in before foaling.

The question of selection of a stallion is twofold: are you selecting a horse to stand at your stud, or are you selecting a stallion suitable to breed to a particular mare? If the former, you want to buy a horse of popular blood lines who will have commercial appeal to other breeders than yourself. Therefore, the rules of selection that apply to any other animal hold here. You've got to have plenty of visible horse and plenty of visible pedigree material showing ability for the job. If the latter, avoid breeding animals that are too closely related, unless you feel sure that you know what you are doing. Remember that when you intensify by using the same sire on both sides of the pedigree you double up a lot of factors, not just one. If you inbreed to one good horse in the pedigree you may find you are also collecting a lot of mediocrity of which you are unaware. I think it is best to stay clear of inbreeding if you can and cross the best stallion that is available with the best mare you have. As John Madden said many years ago, "Breed the best to the best and hope for the best."

Stallions of course need to be handled differently from other horses. They need to be always handled carefully, never abused. Be sure they are getting a lot of exercise, and that they are able to see the countryside when they are turned out. The old European plan of high-walled, solid-fenced paddocks, which leave a horse nothing but four walls to look at, are no good for him at all. The most wonderful stallion setup I know is that long hillside at Claiborne Farm where there are eighteen well-drained, shady stallion paddocks to take care of the horses in the main stallion area.

The question of fertility, of course, is very important. As aforementioned, be sure that fertility is assured if you are buying a horse at auction. It's not the same when you buy an established horse as when you are buying one from racing. A horse who is being sold at auction may not be a good foal getter, so it is up to you to find out all about him from a good reliable source. Also, an established stallion has records available on the number and performance of his progeny whereby you can check his prepotency; in other words, his ability to beget animals similar to himself.

I don't have a very high opinion of so-called nicks, i.e., breeding patterns that have been successful. I think that they are generally caused by propinquity more than anything else. The fact is that more Bull Lea mares were available to Blenheim II because of the ownership of the animals involved: and more Princequillo mares were available to Nasrullah; or again, going way back, there were more Rock Sand mares available to Fair Play than any other line. That had more than anything else to do with establishing the famous "nicks" between these sires and dam's sires mentioned. Furthermore, in the cases cited, the mares were generally of high class, improving prospects for a "nick."

One thing is sure; I want a stallion to look like a stallion just as I want a broodmare to look feminine and not like a stallion. In horses, as in humans, I prefer masculine males and feminine females.

The age of a sire doesn't seem to have much effect upon the quality of his offspring. Though there is some prejudice against old stallions, I wouldn't turn down the foal of a successful, active sire, no matter what his age. Even so, it stands to reason that the younger horse, still in his prime, should have more to pass on to his sons and daughters.

There is more danger in breeding an old mare. Because the mare provides the foal's entire environment and sustenance for eleven months, the foal of an old mare who has lost her condition is very apt to have a weakness, a sort of underdevelopment of which you can say, "well, there's an old mare's child."

Now about selecting yearlings, I prefer young horses that run out and are not stuffed with feed like fat cattle. But rough horses do not bring the big prices. A trainer will say, "Oh, those yearlings are too fat." But which ones does he buy?—the fat ones. If the yearling doesn't have that layer of blubber, buyers will say, "That one must be a poor doer."

Our Fasig-Tipton men frequently visit consignors—try to see as much of their stock as we can. It is not just a matter of looking at horses; we notice whether the breeder is a good "housekeeper," a good feeder, or whether he runs a rough and tumble outfit. If we can get the chance to see the horses running in paddocks, so much the better.

A person buying a yearling should start with the pedigree. In the sales catalogue, he should look for the ones with the most racing quality close up. Every horse in the world has ancestors that have won great races, if you go back far enough, but blood lines may deteriorate or improve from generation to generation. I'd prefer a sire or dam that won its share of good races over a great, great-grandsire that was a world-beater, with every generation going downhill from there. The closer you can get to a Bold Ruler or a Hail to Reason the better off you are—but without investing a lot of money the chances are you won't get very close to that kind.

The first things to look for in a pedigree are: a stallion that is a proven sire, or a top-class young racehorse from a proven family who can be expected to be a good sire; and a dam that was either a first-class racemare, or has been a producer of high-class racehorses. The absolute ideal would be a son of seven-time leading sire Bold Ruler out of a mare such as Somethingroyal, who has produced so many high-class stakes winners. In practice, this is the mating which produced 1973 Triple Crown winner Secretariat. The objective is to get as close as possible to perfection. Some individual horses, male or female, regularly pass along their physical and temperamental qualities to their progeny, regardless of the animals to which they are bred. At Labrot's, I had a mare named White Glade, by White Eagle, out of Eaton Lass. Every year, that mare had a fine-looking foal, and always, her foal was the leader of its group. Her foals generally were good racehorses— always most precocious and always outstanding individuals physically —regardless of the sire. The idea in all breeding is to learn (or attempt to learn) the kind of produce that can be expected from each mare, and the quality a stallion is likely to put into his get.

When a yearling is brought out for inspection, I notice if he comes out smartly, or like a snail. Also, I see if he acts mean or nervous and what general impression he gives. When he approaches, I watch particularly how he walks. If he can't walk, he isn't likely to be able to run. He's got to come to you straight, neither turning his feet out nor in.

No one has been able to devise a yardstick that will measure heart. If we could, we'd probably find great differences in animals in the same group. You have to form your opinion from the expression and poise, or boldness—and the amount of class in the immediate family.

You never know what's hidden inside, though. The physically perfect specimen may prove to be worthless on the racetrack, and the poorly made one might prove to be a star. But you'd better go along with the one with good conformation. In the fifty years that I've been looking over horses, I've found that the outstanding performer or producer usually is a fine individual physically, though it may have minor faults. There is a relationship among class, breeding and conformation. More than likely, the animals with the best credentials are the best looking.

Anyone going into the horse business—either breeding or racing —needs money, intelligence and luck. A combination of any two isn't bad, but having all three is best. I never advise anybody to get into the game, unless he can afford it as a hobby; but what I say isn't going to affect a person who really has the bug. My recommendation is to aim high. If you can get a horse by Bold Ruler out of Somethingroyal— great! If not, get the best you can. Whatever you do, you'll be buying some headaches, but you'll be entering a fascinating game. I only hope you can afford it.

FIFTEEN

Some Horses to Remember

After a man has been looking at horses for more than half a century, and studying them and watching them develop, certain ones always will stand out in memory. They surprise you, disappoint you and thrill you, and make you wonder why they succeeded or failed.

One of the things I remember is Alsab being led into the auction ring at Saratoga in 1940. He was a nice-looking little horse, a trifle low at the withers, maybe, but with no serious faults. By the same token, there was nothing particular to recommend him. He was by Good Goods, which, at that time hadn't got anything, and was a sort of a one-shot horse himself. The market was very bad, so Al Sabath got the colt for $700. Alsab was raced forty-five times in two seasons winning twelve stakes and $110,000 at two, and eight stakes including the Preakness at three. In spite of the way he was handled, he was champion of his generation for two seasons, and a great racehorse. He developed into a good-looking, well-balanced stallion—far different from the animal that had appeared in the sales ring.

Willis Sharpe Kilmer, of Court Manor Stud, New Market, Virginia, used to sell his yearlings at Saratoga. In 1937, he consigned a big brown colt, by Sun Beau, and a little chestnut filly, by Gino, and another one I don't even remember. None of them was sold. Kilmer had placed reserve bids on them, and they went back to him. I looked them over and rejected the filly because she had sickle hocks and a slight hernia and was parrot-mouthed. The big brown colt didn't particularly appeal to me. Bud Stotler bought the three of them for Alfred Vanderbilt, and took them to California. The filly, Galley Slave, won her first three starts at two and set a track record of 33⅖ for three furlongs. She won the 1938 Santa Barbara Stakes, beating colts. The "hernia" was just a superficial blemish and amounted to nothing. Retired to stud, Galley Slave produced several good winners, including stakes winners, none of them parrot-mouthed.

In the spring of 1946, I was down in Kentucky to collect a carload of horses, mostly broodmares, for members of the Maryland Horse Breeders Association. While at Hamburg Place, the old Madden farm, I saw a filly being galloped around a pasture, and it was a nice-moving filly. I looked her over pretty well and asked the man there, "What is it?"

"It's one of Gay Drake's two-year-olds," he answered. "It's down here to be broken."

"Is it for sale?" I asked.

"I don't know," the man replied. "See the farm manager."

So I hollered up to the manager, and he said, "Oh, yes. Mr. Drake is selling all his horses."

I went over the filly again and inquired, "What's he asking for her?"

"$3,500," the man said.

"Oh, hell," I said. "Anything that can gallop is worth $3,500 today!"

Horses were in short supply at that time, so I called Gay and asked, "What about that filly you've got?" (Her name was Black Pine. She was by Sweep Like, out of Black Plane.) "If I can get her to Maryland," I said, "I can sell her. I've got a car going up tomorrow and I've got an empty stall on it. I know I can move her."

Drake said okay, so I called Danny Shea. "I've got a filly named

Black Pine," I told him. "I saw her galloping, and she's got a hell of a nice way of going. The price is only $3,500." I gave him the breeding. Danny said, "Otts Nyberg wants a horse. I'll put him on to her. Bring her along."

Nyberg's wife's name was Iris, so the first thing Nyberg did after he bought her was to change the filly's name to Irisen (pronounced Iris-N)—against my advice. When you change a horse's name it seems to be the kiss of death. I remember Labrot changed the name of a horse, and, the next time it ran, it broke its leg and had to be destroyed.

The name change didn't hex Irisen, though. She did very well and was a stakes winner of over $100,000. Nyberg gave me one of her shoes and I made an ashtray of it which I still have. When she was through racing, Vanderbilt bought Irisen and she was the dam of the stakes winner Idolater. What originally attracted me to Irisen was the way she went, galloping easily in the field, and the picture of her fine action stays with me.

Frank McMahon's Derby-Preakness winner of 1969, Majestic Prince, was considered by many people an almost perfect example of Thoroughbred conformation, and that he was. I knew him well, because Fasig-Tipton sold his dam, Gay Hostess, as a two-year-old, to Leslie Combs II in a Mayer sale. Gay Hostess was injured and never raced. She was a very good-looking mare, and was descended from Boudoir II's family, like Your Host. They all were animals of quality —not big, but beautifully made.

Bred to Raise A Native, Gay Hostess produced Majestic Prince in 1966. At the Keeneland Sales, Frank McMahon got him for $250,000, a record for a yearling colt at the time. Majestic Prince was the first yearling I ever saw that sold for a quarter of a million. He looked like half a million. He was an outstanding foal, an outstanding weanling and an outstanding yearling. When they took the weanlings from their mothers and put them out together, this colt was the leader. When they separated the yearling colts from the fillies, he was the leader of the colts. It wasn't just a physical thing. It was personality and assurance. McMahon saw him on the farm several times. Trainer Johnny Longden didn't see him until the colt was being made ready for the sales. John was crazy about him—wanted him badly—and Longden has seen and ridden many a good horse.

McMahon owned a half interest in the colt, so when it went into the sale he was bidding fifty-cent dollars. That was perfectly legitimate, but it doubled the difficulty of the task of the underbidder, Mrs. Bert Martin, who was offering two dollars for every one bid by McMahon.

In the 1970 Keeneland Sales, McMahon bought Majestic Prince's full brother for $510,000 on the same terms. In every way, that yearling was just a bit better looking than his older brother. Lady Beaverbrook had given me the authority to go to $425,000 for the colt, but that wasn't enough. Thirty seconds after the bidding started, I was out of business. Howard Sams, Indianapolis publisher and owner of Waldemar Farms, Williston, Florida, was hoping to get a worthy stallion prospect. He offered $450,000. Arnold Winick's bid of $5,000 more brought laughs. The crowd was geared to $100,000 steps. Then, McMahon got into the action. His initial bid was $500,000. Winick pushed up the figure another $5,000, but when McMahon said, "Ten," the bidding was over. Named Crowned Prince, the colt was sent to England to be trained. He displayed brilliant class at two under the tutelage of Newmarket trainer Bernard van Cutsem, and was being readied for a classic campaign at three when throat trouble ended his racing career. Syndicated for stud at a value of $1,200,000, he now stands in Ireland under the management of Captain A. D. D. "Tim" Rogers.

Majestic Prince, as a yearling, stood out over his contemporary, the future Belmont Stakes winner, Arts and Letters, who was under trainer Elliott Burch's careful handling. They were entirely different types. They didn't look like the same breed, but the quality was there in both. Arts and Letters developed from month to month and from race to race during the brilliant three-year-old campaign which earned him Horse of the Year honors. In New York, when he won the Belmont Stakes over Majestic Prince, he was a lot more horse in size and shape than he had been the previous winter at Hialeah.

Arts and Letters is by Ribot, and Ribot was a sire that could get a giant like Graustark, or a pony like Ribocco, or Tom Rolfe. He got all sizes and shapes—no uniformity, but loads of class. The best-looking of all Ribot's sons was a horse we bred at Cain Hoy and cast aside as a yearling. That was Ragusa. Captain Harry Guggenheim sent the mare, Fantan, to Italy to be bred to Ribot, then sent her to Ireland, where she foaled Ragusa at Mrs. Muriel McCall's Tally Ho Stud. Captain Cecil Boyd-Rochefort, the famous trainer, saw him and didn't like him, said he was "a little weed." Indeed, Ragusa was an underdeveloped, very backward, unattractive sort of a young one, so he was put in the Dublin yearling sales. Paddy Prendergast saw something in him he liked and bought him for 1,500 guineas.

The colt furnished out well and became a real looker. On the course, he was highly successful. He won the Irish Sweeps Derby, King George VI and Queen Elizabeth Stakes, St. Leger, Eclipse and Great Voltigeur Stakes, at three, and the Sandown Eclipse Stakes at four. As a sire he achieved real success as well.

Ribot, himself, was a handsomely made horse—not a big horse, but deep through the heart, with quality shining in his dark brown coat. He proved his ability on the course by beating everything that was thrown at him—and easily. He was also a horse of temperament. In the stall, he was a perfect gentleman to handle. But, if he got mad, look out! He couldn't be turned out if there was another horse in sight, and he couldn't be turned out in a paddock by himself. A man would have to be there to keep an eye on him. He'd get mad about something and try to tear the place apart.

One day, I took a group of Australians to see Ribot at Darby Dan and, while they were there, some cattle in a neighboring field came over where he could see them. Ribot went into a real fit, reared up on his hind legs and tried to chop down a tree with his front hoofs. Boyd-Rochefort, a great trainer, said, "I wouldn't train a Ribot—wouldn't have one in my yard." That was before Ribot had sired any winners. All of us—even the most brilliant—have our prejudices.

Kelso's feats on the course will always keep his memory alive in the minds of racing folk, but the fact that he came into existence at all is as remarkable as his racing record. Your Host, his sire, fell in the 1951 running of the San Pasqual Handicap, at Santa Anita, and smashed the elbow of the right front leg. Owner William Goetz had insured Your Host with Lloyd's of London for $250,000. For days, agents of Lloyd's and veterinarians debated his fate, while a representative of the A.S.P.C.A. kept close watch over the proceedings. It was touch and go as to whether or not he'd have to be destroyed. Because of the extent of the injury, doctors felt that surgery was out of the question.

The horse's condition was considered so grave that Lloyd's paid off, and took possession of the horse, and initiated a unique rehabilitation program.

Your Host wasn't ready to die. He saved himself by learning to keep his weight off his injured leg. Heat treatments and massages helped. The healing was not "neat," but the horse was saved, and, in eight or nine months, he was looking for some kind of action.

Your Host had run into trouble long before he ever got to the racetrack. As a yearling, he had managed to bang himself up in an accident that nearly cost him his life and left him with a crook in his neck. In running he carried his head low and turned slightly to one side. One eye was lower than the other. Goetz had bought Your Host, as a two-year-old, out of the Mayer sale in January 1949. He paid only $20,000, because of the colt's apparent physical imperfections, but he got a bargain, and he got a runner—a horse of brilliant speed. He won the Del Mar Futurity, California Breeders' Champion Stakes, Santa Anita Derby, Kent and Dick Welles Stakes, and the Golden State Breeders', Thanksgiving Day and Santa Catalina Handicaps. In the Catalina, he carried 130 pounds and went a mile and one-eighth in 1:48⅕. Then came his dreadful accident.

To Lloyd's, Your Host was like a wrecked ship that had been salvaged. Whatever they could get for him was salvage value as against what they had paid out for him. They sent him up to George Stratton's Circle S Ranch, at Canoga Park, California, where he served part of a season at stud.

With an underwriter of Lloyd's I went to look over the horse. We were astonished at his ability to handle himself. The thing that struck me about him was his courage—his determination to keep going. He wouldn't die; he wouldn't give in. I was so impressed, I knew he had to be a sire. And he was.

I had a good talk with the man who had been taking care of Your Host, and I also talked with the veterinarian, Dr. Jack Baker. Then, I offered to take an option on the horse. Lloyd's approved this and I got the option. The figure agreed upon was $150,000.

First, I offered Your Host to Californians. I figured they had a right to him. He was a California-bred, and he was a god in the State. To Louis Rowan, president of the California Thoroughbred Breeders'

Association, I offered first option at $150,000; but the breeders of the State couldn't get together.

When I got back East, I told F. Wallis Armstrong, Jr., about Your Host. Wally had had polio, which had affected the use of a hand and arm. He was very interested in the horse, because he and Your Host had both overcome handicaps. He said he'd like to see if he could get a syndicate together in New Jersey.

Armstrong did get some people together, but they wouldn't give $150,000 for the horse in California. They *would* pay $150,000 for him delivered safely in New Jersey. We worked out a compromise. We made the price $140,000 and Armstrong's group assumed the responsibility of transportation. Lloyd's accepted the deal, and the horse was shipped to Meadowview Farm.

The curious thing was that, in the small crop Your Host got in California, there were three stakes winners, Miss Todd, Blen Host and Social Climber. All of his get were better than average.

Then the next thing you know, along comes Kelso—the best—the champion who was sired in New Jersey. An early injury which delayed his training cost him his chance to participate in the classics, but he soon established his class and was Horse of the Year at three and for the next four years, which was absolutely phenomenal, and he earned $1,977,896, still the record earned by a horse.

In 1961, when he was fourteen years old, Your Host injured his right stifle, after he had been bred to four mares. The rest of his book of twenty-seven was canceled. Again, a jury convened to determine the question of life or death. Actually, there wasn't much to debate. Crippled as he was in his right foreleg, he was in a sad plight with his right hind leg useless. Your Host had survived two serious hurts, either of which might have ended the career of a horse of less determination, but this time the bell tolled. Veterinarians found that all of what you might call the "joint oil" was all gone. How the hell he had kept going in his later days, I don't know. It was incredible.

The only humane thing to do was to end his suffering. Your Host was buried at Meadowview Farm alongside Easton and Man o' War's greatest rival, John P. Grier.

Bahram, Mahmoud and Blenheim II were horses that impressed me. A big, rangy, dark brown horse, Bahram won the English Triple

Crown of Two Thousand Guineas, Epsom Derby and St. Leger, in 1935. And that feat wasn't repeated until Nijinsky completed the sweep in 1970. Bahram was the second Epsom Derby winner for the Aga Khan. Blenheim II was the first, winning in 1930, and Mahmoud was the third, in 1936. Blenheim II was imported to America in 1936 and the other two followed in 1940.

Bahram, like Blenheim II, was by Blandford. His dam was Friar's Daughter, by Friar Marcus, a great speed sire. Unbeaten in nine starts as a two- and three-year-old, Bahram begot a number of good stakes winners in England before being purchased by Walter P. Chrysler, Sylvester W. Labrot, Alfred G. Vanderbilt and James Cox Brady, who brought him to America. The price, I believe, was $160,000.

Bahram stood at Chrysler's North Wales Stud, at Warrenton, Virginia, and, later, at Alfred Vanderbilt's Sagamore Farm, Glyndon, Maryland. He had a world of eye appeal, and made a tremendous impression on the observer, but the thought struck me that he never would do for America—because of his make and shape. He was too big and leggy; and the same thing was true of Cain Hoy's Bald Eagle, who I always thought would have done much better in France. This opinion was at least partially borne out, in 1972, when Bald Eagle's daughter, San San, out of a Cain Hoy mare, won France's Prix Vermeille and Prix de l'Arc de Triomphe, and was European filly of the year. Bahram probably paid off, though. He sired Stud Poker, Sun Bahram, one good horse for Brady, a decent filly for Vanderbilt, and a nice colt, Bovard, for Sylvester Labrot, Jr. I think each member of the purchasing group got at least one worthwhile runner.

In 1945, Bahram was sold to Señor Miguel Martinez de Hoz, and moved to that gentleman's stud, Chapadmalal, near Buenos Aires, in the Argentine, but he wasn't destined to do any real good there either. Despite his less-than-spectacular stud work, Bahram remains in my mind's eye as a horse of great quality and scope, and he was a superior racehorse.

Mahmoud was not quite so good on the course, but he had beautiful balance, tremendous speed. By Blenheim II, he was a gray of medium size who bounced like a cork. He won the Epsom Derby on a very fast track. The turf was hard, and he scored in a record time of 2:33⅘ for the mile and a half. That figure was equaled by Airborne in

1947, but had not been surpassed up to 1970. (Faster times were registered at Newmarket, during the years of World War II, where the race was staged as "The New Derby Stakes.")

Cornelius Vanderbilt Whitney imported Mahmoud. According to reports he paid $84,000 for him. A foal of 1933, Mahmoud was a year younger than Bahram, smaller and more compact, more like a polo pony, or an American speed horse. You looked at him and you knew he was going to "fit," because you could breed him to any kind of mare.

Blenheim II, Mahmoud's sire, was not so strongly characterized a horse as Mahmoud. Each was about fifteen hands, three inches—maybe Blenheim II was half an inch taller, but he wasn't so robust or so masculine a horse as Mahmoud. When Blenheim II was brought to this country in 1936, the year Mahmoud won the Epsom Derby, American breeders and writers about breeding were highly enthusiastic about the acquisition. Most believed he would be a factor in the never-ending objective of "improving the breed."

Herr Friedrich Becker, the distinguished German authority, was of a different mind. In a letter to me, he described Blenheim II as "a marish sort of horse, which—this you may take from me—will prove a ghastly failure." Anyone wishing to make an ass of himself has only to issue an unqualified statement about a racehorse. The horse will take it from there. Blenheim II sired five winners of over $200,000, among them, Whirlaway, leading money winner up to his time with $561,161, and a Triple Crown winner; Fervent, an American Derby winner; and Thumbs Up, victor in the Santa Anita Handicap. Also among his progeny were many fine fillies that turned out to be first-rate producers, including the dams of Kentucky Derby winners Hill Gail, Kauai King, top runners Coaltown and Mark-Ye-Well, and great producers, Wistful and Prophet's Bell.

Blenheim II always had top-class mares. The Aga Khan bought superior fillies and Blenheim II never was bred to anything that was short of first-rate. In this country the same thing happened. The people who brought him over sent their best mares to him.

Mahmoud became America's leading sire of 1946, and for eight successive years was among our ten leading sires. In addition, he joined the ranks of leading brood mare sires in 1954, topped that roster in 1957, and was among the ten leaders thirteen times in a fifteen-year span.

Sir Gallahad was another imported stallion who was always bred to the best available mares. When Sir Gallahad III came over, eight people had shares in him—William Woodward and A. B. Hancock among them. All of them had the finest stock. They would breed their own mares to the horse, or swap services with the owner of another top-class stallion. In either case Sir Gallahad would be bred to a good mare.

Man o' War was a phenomenal sire, particularly considering the mares that were bred to him. If Man o' War had had the same chances as Sir Gallahad III, at the same time, it is impossible to imagine what his record might have been. But old man Riddle (Samuel D. Riddle) built a fence around Man o' War. Liz Whitney got to breed a mare or two to him, but other than that, the only ones sent to him were Riddle's own and some of those owned by Walter M. Jeffords, husband of Mrs. Riddle's niece.

From a Star Shoot mare Man o' War got Crusader, and from a Sweep mare he got War Admiral. So Riddle went around collecting all the Star Shoot and Sweep mares he could lay his hands on, and a lot of them were simply worthless. The great turf journalist, Joe Palmer, wrote "Whirlaway was bred to more distinguished mares in one year than Man o' War was in ten." Yet, in spite of being restricted, for the most part, to mediocre mates, Man o' War led the stallion list in 1926 in money won, and, almost every season during his term of service at stud, he was represented on the track by horses of top class. American Flag, Crusader, Mars, Scapa Flow, Genie and Clyde Van Dusen, and the fillies Bateau and Edith Cavell, were in his first five crops. War Admiral and War Relic came along later. Then, there was Battleship, winner of the Liverpool Grand National, and Blockade, the great timber horse, three-time winner of the Maryland Hunt Cup. What Man o' War would have been as a progenitor under the handling of Arthur B. Hancock, there's no telling. He was phenomenal as it was, but he would have been greater yet.

Secretariat, the "super horse" and Triple Crown winner of 1973, has valid credentials and many supporters as claimant to "horse of the century" laurels. Winner of the Kentucky Derby and Belmont Stakes in record times, and the Preakness in a disputed near-record performance which may well have beaten the old standard, Secretariat dominated the three-year-old picture as no horse had since Citation. Whether he measures up to Man o' War as a sire will be a number of years in the learning.

In my opinion, Man o' War was the greatest horse we've ever had. There just hasn't been anything to compare with him—even Citation. Many a time I argued that point with Ben and Jimmy Jones. I saw Citation run many times, and was very close to him. He was great, and there haven't been many better. But when you're talking about the greatest, you can't judge horses that are standing before you. You have to stand back and let the years roll by. Then you can see the highlights. You can judge by the impression each great horse made on the people who were watching him.

Physically, Man o' War was a robust individual with very strong bone. He wasn't a "quality" horse, he was a big, rugged, heavyweight-boxer type. He carried his head higher than most horses do, and was simply the picture of immense strength, ruggedness and character—always.

Andrew Jackson Joyner, one of the most brilliant trainers of his or any era in America and in England, declared that there was no horse like Man o' War. He told me that Man o' War was the only horse he ever saw that was allowed to run all-out only once or twice and then only for a short distance—the only horse that could break a watch every day he went out on the racetrack, if they'd let him. "In all my life," said Joyner, "I've never seen a horse like him."

SIXTEEN

And Some
Friends

We all know that, some day for each of us there'll be "one clear call," and away we go. Death is inevitable, but the death of a dear friend brings sorrow and a sense of loss. There always is "moaning at the bar," because people always are dying, but it's something you can't get used to, or be casual about. Almost automatically, you remember experiences and laughs you had with the one that's gone, and, forever, there'll be times when you'll think of him and wish he were back to do them all over again.

There is something about the horse that establishes a fraternity among men. For one thing, there's no problem about a topic of conversation. The word "horse" starts it and it goes on and on and on. It's the same in every stratum of the horse world—in the barns and the manor houses, and on the racetracks. Traveling all over America and in other lands, I have met thousands of people and made lasting friendships that I consider my richest treasures. Some of the friends have passed on, others are still around, and many will outlast me.

Anyone who is in the horse business for more than a week has to make the acquaintance of at least one veterinarian. For the ten years that I was at Labrot's, my nearest DVM was thirty miles away. The one I called on most was Dr. Harry A. Meisner, who had his headquarters in Towson, Maryland, north of Baltimore. Dr. Meisner was an old-time trotting-horse man. In his early years of practice, he had "cut his teeth" on streetcar-line horses, brewers' horses, cab horses, and the various other equines that were working on the cobblestone streets of Baltimore. That experience had given him a wonderful knowledge of horses' feet. Besides, it made him fully aware of all the things that can happen to a horse, and the troubles an animal can make for himself and those who are looking after him.

Doc Meisner had two identifying properties—his old Packard car and his cigars. He always carried a box of cigars in the auto. Before examining a patient, he went through the ritual of taking a cigar himself and handing one to any cigar-smokers who were working with him. Then he was ready.

He always insisted upon a quiet approach. He would stand outside a stall door for several minutes, just observing the animal, regardless of what its problem might be. He wanted no one in the stall pulling the horse around. He just wanted to look and form his own conclusions on the basis of what he saw. Then, he would go in and go to work.

Over the years, Doc Meisner and I developed a system of communication that was good for both of us. It saved him mileage and I acquired considerable education in the field of veterinary medicine. I would phone him and describe the symptoms, and he would tell me what he thought the trouble was, and prescribe the course I should follow—what medicine to give and what treatment to apply. In the evening, or, perhaps, the next day, I'd call him again to report the condition of the animal and he'd give further orders. If the horse showed no improvement (or got worse), the doctor would come down, and give the horse his personal attention.

Doc Meisner was well known and respected throughout his orbit of activity, for being both a good horseman and a good veterinarian. The world of veterinary science has changed a lot since his day, but those who knew him remember him with affection. He was wonderful to me, and taught me many things. He was helpful to everyone who had the privilege of his acquaintanceship. Unfortunately, he did not lay aside much in the way of worldly goods. When he passed away, he left only his house and its furnishings, plus thirty suits and fifteen over-coats. I bought his desk and his desk chair, and they have served for more than thirty years.

Another veterinarian who left a lasting impression with me was H. A. Woodroofe, M.R.C.V.S. (Member of the Royal College of Veteri-nary Surgeons). Dr. Woodroofe had been attached to the British Army during the Afghan Wars in the early '80s, so he was well practiced when he arrived in America. He came, at the request of the United States Government, to deal with a type of pneumonia that had showed up in beef cattle in the Bourbon-and-Scott-County area of Kentucky. When he first started practicing in the U.S., he wore a top hat and frock coat and regular formal attire, and he employed a Negro lad to drive his horse and buggy and carry his bag.

Sad to say, it was his wont to take trips on the alcohol train. At various periods during his career, he was completely down and out. There were times when the city of Lexington provided him with room and board, but didn't give him the key. Once, after spending the winter in the Lexington workhouse, he sent the city a bill for professional services rendered for treatment of cattle and mules on the workhouse farm. City spokesmen maintained that he had been their guest all winter and they figured it was an even deal. The doctor went to court and the judge ruled that the city had to pay.

I acquired a number of Woodroofe's books, among them Leeney's *Veterinary Horse Medicine.* In that book there are some interesting mar-ginal notes and a prescription or two written on blank pages. Inside the back cover I found the following "hop" formula, recorded fifty-odd years ago:

Heroin H.C.L. 12 grains

Aromatic spirits of ammonia 6 fluid ounces

Caffeine alkaloid 6 ounces

Spirits of nitroglycerin 2 ounces

Strychnine 6 grains

Brandy or alcohol, quantity sufficient to make one quart

The horse was supposed to toss off two ounces of this, with a water chaser, half an hour before post time. How effective the dose would be, I never have attempted to ascertain. My guess is that the horse would go on a pretty good trip, but something might show up in the chemical tests to arouse the suspicions of the laboratory technicians.

For some years, Woodroofe was on Easy Street, because Lloyd's of London required that every veterinary certificate be signed by an M.R.C.V.S. when they insured a horse. As Doc was the only one that qualified in the Bluegrass Country of Kentucky, he made a living just by signing papers. Now that rule has been changed, and the signature of any veterinarian in good standing is acceptable to Lloyd's Underwriters.

Woodroofe was our guest at Holly Beach Farm for long stays several times. Once he was with us for about a year, and then vanished. He was a man of vast experience, and associating with him was extremely beneficial to me. It is a tragic experience to see a man of brilliance go down the hill, a victim of one besetting weakness.

Another vet who has shared his knowledge with me and helped me in many ways is Dr. William R. McGee, a leader in the field of equine gynecology. But when thinking of doctors of veterinary medicine, I suppose the one who impressed me most by word and deed was Charles Blackhurst. I was a mere lad when I tagged along with him as he went his rounds. With him, I learned something of the work of the vet, and how important it is to have one available when you're dealing with horses. I wonder today at the man's patience, performing his work and answering the questions of an overly curious youngster. Perhaps it was because he saw that I was deeply interested that he was so liberal with his time and knowledge.

Admiral Cary T. Grayson was a man who helped me and was an inspiration. An M.D., he was the personal physician of President Woodrow Wilson, and had a tremendous responsibility in that capacity for a number of years. A native Virginian, full of stories about his beloved state, Admiral Grayson developed a great interest in Thoroughbred breeding and became an avid student of bloodlines. He acquired High Time, and later stood Happy Argo at his Blue Ridge Stud, in Virginia. Until his untimely death, the Admiral looked after the turf affairs of Robert Sterling Clark. Admiral Grayson could "walk with kings—nor lose the common touch." I remember so well sitting with him, far back in Laurel's grandstand, and talking about horses.

Holly Beach was importing Kantar at the time, and the Admiral was interested in the stallion's potential. Following our conversation, he sent a mare to Kantar. Unfortunately, the horse never did anybody any good, except that his yearlings sold well for a couple of years. He did sire one or two good broodmares.

Another man who extended a helping hand to me was John W. Hanes, of the New York Racing Association. Mr. Hanes helped with the reorganization of Fasig-Tipton when I went with the company in 1952. Then in 1954, when I had my heart attack and needed strength on the board, he accepted a directorship. His advice was always invaluable in the operation of the company.

In January 1958, the Breeders' Sales Company of Lexington, Kentucky, announced that George Swinebroad had been named vice-president in charge of field activities. The agreement specified that George sever his connections with other Thoroughbred sales companies. That meant that he would have to terminate his long-time relationship with Fasig-Tipton, after the dispersal of the estate of Louis B. Mayer—the last Mayer sale—on January 6.

I was sorry that circumstances made it necessary for our ways to part. A superb auctioneer, a fine man and a good friend, George always has been a credit to his profession. I gave him his first job as an auctioneer of Thoroughbreds. It happened in Maryland in the fall of 1939. I was reorganizing the Maryland Breeders' sales for Timonium, and we wanted Doc Bond, one of the best, to auction for us. Doc was under contract to Fasig-Tipton Company, then owned by Mrs. E. J. Tranter, who refused to let him sell for us. I made a phone call to Joe Estes, then editor of *The Blood-Horse*, in Lexington, to ask for suggestions. Estes told me of a fellow who had shown ability in auctioning Standardbreds—a chap named George Swinebroad, for whom he predicted a great future. I never had heard of the man, but I respected Estes' judgment in all things, and wired George asking him to call me. Sight unseen, I hired him over the phone, and he worked the sale with me. I can't estimate the value of the horses we sold together in the twenty years that followed.

Swinebroad always said that the first Louis B. Mayer sale was the greatest in the annals of recorded racing, not only for the prices obtained, but for tenseness, suspense, and pure drama. Since that time, there were sales that were lollapaloozas, but I'm inclined to agree with George. It is hard to find words to describe that sale. It was like a movie.

Danny Shea was an amazing man. When he was just fourteen, he jumped a horse seven feet, one inch in the Clinton, Massachusetts horse show. Two years later, he sent Tipperary over a seven-foot, nine-inch jump at Reedville, Mass., almost equaling the world record. From 1934 to '36, Danny gained fame as a rider of high-jump horses. With Little Squire, he won the jumping championship at Madison Square Garden two years in a row. Little Squire was very small, not much bigger than a pony. Danny bought him for $225 and sold him five years later when the horse was eighteen for $3,500.

Danny managed M. Robert Guggenheim's Firenze Stable. He got into training Thoroughbreds, and, about 1936, decided that he wanted to buy a farm. Danny and his wife Martha (Marty) asked me to find a place for them in Maryland. They wanted sixty or eighty acres. At that time, William Elder, whom I knew very well, was trying to dispose of his farm—about 200 acres, ideally situated near Hyde, Maryland. I called Danny and told him about it. He said that 200 acres was too much; he couldn't afford to buy it.

"You can't afford *not* to buy this place," I told him. "You've got to buy it, because you can get it for $20,000, and for practically nothing down."

Then I called Bill Elder, and explained that I had a man in Boston who wanted to buy the place. "He'll give the $20,000 you're asking," I said, "but he doesn't have much cash."

"How much can he put down?" Mr. Elder asked.

"Oh," I said, "about a thousand."

"Well," said Elder, "if you say he's the right kind of a guy and a horseman, I'll take a mortgage for the rest."

"Okay," I said, "it's a deal."

Danny and Marty immediately came down to have a look at the farm. Marty's mother thought it was terrible, and the house *was* terrible. But I said, "Look at the barns, and the land you're getting. You can fill up this place with the boarders you've got up in Dover." Danny was renting a small farm in Massachusetts, that was overflowing with the horses he was boarding. "Bring 'em all down and you'll pay for this farm with the fees you're getting," I insisted.

Danny and Marty realized they were getting a real good deal. (Merryland Farm must have been worth ten times as much in '59 when Danny died and twenty times as much in 1973.) I called Elder and told him the Sheas were going to take the place. Then I called his real estate broker, explained who I was and said, "I've just sold Merryland Farm."

"Oh," the man said, "I'm taking someone out to look at it tomorrow."

"Don't bother," I said. "It's sold."

"I don't understand," the broker persisted.

"Ask Bill Elder," I advised.

The outcome was that I took Danny and Marty in my car down to Charles Street and Cold Spring Lane in Baltimore, where we met the broker and settled the transaction on a street corner. All the time, the real estate man was saying, "This is very irregular," and "This is all out of line—doing business like this." Irregular or not, it was legal, and the Sheas acquired a wonderful Thoroughbred farm.

Gerald McElligott, MRCVS and a director of the British Bloodstock Agency, managed Robert Sterling Clark's affairs in England as I did in America, so we had frequent contacts. Gerald was responsible for Mr. Clark's breeding Never Say Die—mating Nasrullah with Singing Grass. Also, it was Gerald who insisted upon running Never Say Die in the Epsom Derby. Mr. Clark had no idea the colt was going to run. His instructions to McElligott were, "it's up to you." McElligott also advised Mr. Clark to give Never Say Die to the English National Stud, with the condition that ten nominations be available to ten different Irish breeders annually.

Earlier, Gerald had picked out Nasrullah and bought him for Mr. Joseph McGrath. In company with "Doctor Dolittle," famous British Turf scribe, he first saw Nasrullah as a foal at the side of Mumtaz Begum, at the Egerton Stud, Newmarket, where the Aga Khan's breeding stock was stabled at that time. Looking at the baby horse, McElligott said, "That's the greatest mover I ever saw. Did you ever see the like of him? I'm off to the War. Watch him and let me know how he develops."

Later, when Nasrullah was at stud near Newmarket and had earned a reputation for being something approaching a man-eater, McElligott went to have a look at him. He couldn't find anyone to show him the horse, so, though badly crippled, he went into the box alone.

By the time the stud groom came along, he had gone over Nasrullah thoroughly, before and behind. From this experience, he was convinced that the stories about the horse's ferocity were exaggerated, and bought him for Mr. McGrath for about $24,000. Later, Nasrullah was sold to an American group for about a quarter of a million dollars.

Ben A. Jones died on June 13, 1961, at the age of seventy-eight, and his death really left me feeling empty. He had been a close personal friend for many years. Around Ben, something always was happening, and he had the most picturesque ways of describing things. "When I was a boy," he said, "I was crazy about horses and Holstein cows. I couldn't decide which I liked better. When I got big enough to help with the milking, I knew right away."

Ben was a bug on well-fleshed horses. He sent 'em out round and sleek. He believed that in a long campaign a horse had to have a reserve to call upon, and his sensational successes with Thoroughbreds showed the wisdom of his methods. He'd look at a horse in training and say, "Well, what do we do with this one? We've worked him too much. Just give him the 'easy' today." Of another, he'd say, "This one is on his toes, you'd better let him go a half in forty-eight," or something like that.

Whirlaway belonged to Calumet Farm, but he was Ben Jones's horse. With some other trainer the 1941 Triple Crown winner might have turned out to be an incorrigible rascal. Ben was patient and thorough. On Wednesday morning, during the week after Whirly had won the Kentucky Derby, I was walking across the infield at Pimlico, and Jones was marching Whirlaway from one hurdle to another and allowing him to have a look.

"B.A.," I asked, "what the hell are you doing?"

He said, "If I don't show this dumb son-of-a-bitch everything that's here, he's apt to stop on Saturday and have a look at it. I'm going to be damn sure he's seen everything there is to see and knows what it is, before he gallops tomorrow and breezes Thursday. 'Cause, with him, you never know what he'll do." (That year, in case anyone is thinking of looking it up, the Preakness was run on May 10, just one week after the Derby.)

Whirlaway's performance in the Preakness was dramatic. The race is at 1¾₆ miles, and when the field went into the clubhouse turn, the

newsreel men on the roof had to swing their cameras back to pick up
Whirlaway. He was ten or a dozen lengths behind the next-to-last
horse. Somewhere on the backstretch he was in the middle of things,
and at the far turn he was flying. I still can see his long tail streaming
out in the wind, and Arcaro whaling him. He passed King Cole on the
final bend and was a length and a half in front going by the starting
gate. From there on, he widened out his margin and won by five and
a half. Whirlaway went on to win the Belmont in a gallop, at one to
four, and later became the leading money-winner of the world with
$561,161, which doesn't seem much by present-day standards, but hay
was a lot cheaper in those days.

B. A. was a kindly man, and an absolute genius as a trainer. He
could tell a horse's condition by looking at him, and watching his
actions. He *knew*, and all his men and boys swore by him. And he
depended a lot on what they told him. What he did with the Calumet
horses over the period of the stable's greatness was little short of
fantastic. Five times, the stable had the Horse of the Year—Whirlaway
twice, Twilight Tear, Armed and Citation. In 1947, Calumet had the
best two-year-old filly, Bewitch; the best juvenile colt, Citation; and the
best handicap horse, Armed. Ben saddled six Kentucky Derby winners
(though Jimmy, his son, must be given much of the credit for Citation).
Jimmy saddled Citation for his Preakness and Belmont wins. The
Louisville winners were Lawrin (for Herbert Woolf), Whirlaway, Pen-
sive, Ponder, Citation and Hill Gail.

Some of the terms Ben used in expressing himself were not in the
dictionary, but no one needed an interpreter to understand them. Of
a very fast horse, he would say, "He runs like a hant." I never asked
him what a "hant" was, but I suppose it was a "haunt" or ghost; but
when he said that, I knew the horse could run like blazes. "That's his
holt," Ben would say, when he'd found a horse's best distance or style
of running. No explanation needed. About turf racing, Ben often said,
"Every horse runs on the grass before he runs on the dirt."

Ben was a realist, and never was impressed when some blue-tailed
wonder won six in a row. "If they run often enough, they all get beat,"
Ben would say, and history supports this observation.

Late in life, he said, "Now, I work a lot with young horses. It's really something to watch them develop into stakes winners. Next year's horses, and the hopes you have for them—that's what keeps you young."

A great man, Mister Jones.

SEVENTEEN

Souvenirs

A man in the business of selling horses at public auction for thirty years is certain to collect a gavel or two along the way. One I treasure highly was presented to me at a dinner held by the Saratoga Springs Chamber of Commerce on April 11, 1959. It is a tradition of the Saratoga Chamber of Commerce that a tribute be paid to a business that has contributed to the city's well-being over a period of years. Fasig-Tipton was honored as the Firm of the Year in 1959.

I represented the company and was presented with a gavel made of wood from the balustrade rail of the old Grand Union Hotel. It is beautifully turned, and finished with a silver band. I have used it to open the Saratoga Sales in the years since, but I always use it tenderly, as this is a special memento. The bannister from which it was carved was caressed by the hand of Lillian Russell as she and Diamond Jim Brady went up the stairs to their suites. You have to feel sentimental about something like that.

On January 24, 1967, I received an award from the Thoroughbred

Owners and Breeders' Association who publish *The Blood-Horse*, in recognition of having contributed to the magazine for over twenty-seven years. The award, made in Miami, was a silver tray to which was attached one of the shoes worn by Buckpasser in winning The Jockey Club Gold Cup. I received another award that year, the Distinguished Horseman's Award, given by the Horse Science School of the University of Wisconsin, at River Falls. This was in token of contributions to the horse industry over the years. Also in 1967, I was elected vice-president of the Thoroughbred Club.

At Yakima, Washington, in December '68, Lee Eaton, Dr. "Mickey" Prickett and I were programed on the Stud Manager's Course. Wherever offered, the course has been a tremendous success. And the response in Washington was gratifying. Dr. Edouard Pouret, the leading veterinarian in France, was there and also addressed the group. While in Yakima I was presented with a bronze plaque by the Washington Horse Breeders' Association designating me as "The International Horseman of the Decade," quite an honor—and a surprise.

At the end of August 1956, at the Del Mar Sales, I received my "commission" as a Kentucky Colonel. This and $1,251,201 would have bought me Nashua, if I'd had it earlier. It is an honor, though one that is shared with a few million other "colonels."

The presentation was made by George Swinebroad, at the instance of Kentucky Governor A. B. (Happy) Chandler. My oldest brother, Claud William McQuade Stanley Finney, served twenty-five years in the engineering branch of the General Post Office, and eleven years as chief mechanical transport officer of the Ministry of Aviation, and, upon his retirement, was presented with the Order of the British Empire. My younger brother, Philip Edmund Finney, was out in India for twenty years with the Indian Police Service. He was sent to Nyasaland to set up an agency similar to America's Federal Bureau of Investigation, and he too earned the Order of the British Empire. And I end up a Kentucky Colonel.

To spend your life doing what you like to do, and then have your friends get together and tell you they like the way you've been doing it, is a pleasing experience. This happened to me on October 23, 1969, when I was guest of honor at the Annual Dinner of the Thoroughbred Club of America at Keeneland. Four times, I had been master of

ceremonies when others were honored by the TCA, and extolling their
worth to the Thoroughbred industry was easy and pleasant. It is not
false modesty to state that I wondered if I quite "fitted in" with such
distinguished company. Only thirty-seven before me had been singled
out for recognition by the Thoroughbred Club and virtually all of them
were actively engaged in breeding and racing horses.

The dinner was on my 67th birthday, and my records show that
it was the biggest birthday I ever had. About 500 people showed up,
and I received congratulatory telegrams, phone calls and letters from
I don't know how many more. One friend after another rose and said
nice things about me. When they were done, I was almost convinced
that they had the right man after all. Between speeches—I didn't want
to miss any of the complimentary words—my mind went back to that
day in 1921 when I stepped off the boat in New York. Taking that
perspective, I asked myself, "Who'd have thought this ever would
happen to me?" Then, to put the icing on my cake, after everyone else
was through, they let me talk. What a birthday!

Summing up, I'm sure I have omitted many old friends who
should have been included. Unfortunately, on the shady side of seventy the heart remembers but the head sometimes forgets. All the
friends of all the years have made mine a full and satisfying life, and
while the actuaries tell me I have more years to look back on than to
look forward to, I'm not yet ready to pack it in.

One of the lovely qualities of the horse business is its annual
regeneration: next spring is a new foal crop, perhaps with its Man o'
War or Secretariat; next summer is a new draft of sales yearlings. Each
year it's pleasant to get back to the old places, like Saratoga and
Newmarket, for they combine recollections of times past with the bus-
tle of tomorrow's history in the making. But at the same time, if I don't
get back, I hope I have a right to feel that I've given as much to these
old places as they've given to me—that it's been a fair exchange.

Index